52

GREAT MANAGEMENT TIPS

A year of weekly management advice by nationally syndicated
GateHouse Media columnist Eric P. Bloom

By Eric P. Bloom

Forward by GateHouse News Service Executive Editor
Lisa Glowinski

ISBN: 1470126168
ISBN 13: 9781470126162
Library of Congress Control Number: 2012903794
CreateSpace, North Charleston, SC

To Cheryl, my wife and love of my life

ACKNOWLEDGEMENTS

Writing a book of this type—a compilation of weekly columns—is like running a marathon. In a marathon, you initially need permission from the race officials to participate in the event. Then, during the race, you need to be given water each mile to be sure you stay hydrated and on track. Lastly, at the end of the race you need support and encouragement to help you across the finish line.

When writing this book, I first needed the support and trust of those at GateHouse Media, who accepted me as a syndicated columnist. To those at GateHouse I am truly grateful for allowing me to participate within such a great organization. In particular I would like to thank my Executive Editor Lisa Glowinski, not only for her great guidance, assistance, and support during the past year but also for her willingness to write the forward of this book.

Next I would like to thank my readers. You are the ones that make writing the column worthwhile. I hope that my words of wit and wisdom over the past year have been of value to you.

Many thanks, as well, to the many newspaper editors around the country that have chosen to include my column in their newspapers. I truly appreciate your support.

I would also like to thank my proofreaders Harold and Barbara, who have been proofreading my written words for what seems like a lifetime. Your help on my weekly columns and this book have been of immeasurable value.

Lastly, I would like to thank my wife Cheryl, who has spent much of the last year patiently listening to me talk about column topics, column titles, and column content. Her willingness to listen, give support, and provide great suggestions is truly appreciated. Yes, Cheryl, I am a lucky man :)

52 GREAT MANAGEMENT TIPS
By Eric P. Bloom

TABLE OF CONTENTS

Forward

Good management is a journey, not a destination. It takes patience, creativity, willingness to learn, and willingness to fail, among other virtues.

Eric P. Bloom's columns on management recognize that and try to share the experience he's accumulated—the successes and failures, the clever ideas and the ones that weren't so hot—with others at every level of management.

The following book compiles a wealth of tips—many more than 52, in fact—that will be an amazing playbook for a new manager and a superb refresher for anyone who's been the boss for a while.

I believe good managers know that it isn't about them—it's about the staff. Good managers facilitate effective, efficient ways for employees to get their work accomplished successfully. They help employees learn new skills, grow into the workers they want to become, and, yes, enjoy their jobs. Managers stick up for their team, making sure they're treated fairly and respectfully by other departments, as well as within their own crew.

Employees are interesting (read: sometimes difficult), but, overall, they're looking to you to lead them through times of change, ease stressful situations and just make sure their paychecks are on time.

Management, when done well and mindfully, can be exceptionally rewarding.

As Eric signs off each of his columns, "Manage well, manage smart, and continue to grow." This book will help anyone do just that.

Lisa Glowinski

Executive editor, GateHouse News Service, a division of GateHouse Media, publisher of more than 400 community publications and related websites in the U.S.

INTRODUCTION

A friend of mine likes to say, "Management would be great if it wasn't for the people." Well, I do have to admit that managing people would be a lot easier if employees each came with their own user manual, like a cell phone or a TV set. But obviously they don't. Therefore, as managers we have to decide how to best motivate, manage, and lead each individual on our team based on their individual needs, interests, and personas.

In addition to managing our teams, we must also properly communicate upward to our managers, cooperate with our peers, and deal effectively with vendors, internal company clients, and/or external company customers.

Next you have all the management processes that must be formed on an ongoing basis, such as salary planning, budgeting, hiring, performance review writing, and other similar tasks.

Lastly, you have to assure that the business processes within your department are running smoothly.

Wow, doesn't being a manager sound like fun? Well, some days it is and some days it isn't.

When I became a manager, I found that I needed to grow in three ways. I had to:

- Manage my team
- Perform manager-level activities, such as hiring new employees and giving performance reviews
- Participate in company-wide processes, such as budgeting and salary planning

I learned some of these skills on my own through trial and error. The majority of this information, however, was explained to me by the great managers that I had over the years.

In that spirit, then, the goal of my columns with GateHouse Media is to pay forward the kindness and sharing I enjoyed by teaching these management techniques and processes to others. My hope is that this knowledge will help these newer managers and would-be managers become successful in their managerial endeavors.

This book, as the name alludes, is a compilation of a year's worth of weekly columns, organized by topic and enhanced with various thoughts, tips, tricks, stories, and insights.

This book can be used differently based on your current level of management experience. By level, I'm referring to the following categories:

- Individual contributor or future leader/manager
- Developing leader/manager
- Experienced leader/manager
- Executive leader/manager

Please note that I refer to these categories as "leader/manager." I have found that some people are good managers, but not good leaders. Some people are good leaders, but not good managers. There are also, however, some people that are good at both. (Okay, for completeness and correctness, there are also people that are bad managers and bad leaders.)

If you are an individual contributor, consider this book to be a guide to help you prepare for and ultimately assimilate into a future management role.

If you are a developing leader/manager, use this book to gain insights into issues and situations you will eventually encounter as part of your management journey.

If you are an experienced leader/manager, find those specific nuggets of wisdom that will help you expand your management knowledge. The material may also assist you in training the new or soon-to-be managers working for you.

If you are an executive leader/manager, use this book as a way to help maximize your group's management bench strength.

Enjoy the book, manage well, manage smart, and continue to grow.

Eric

FOR THE MANAGER NEWBIE

Imagine that your boss came into your office and said, "Congratulations, because of the great work you have been doing and our confidence in you as a future leader, we are promoting you into a job you did not go to school for, have not been trained in, and for which nothing in your current role has prepared you. Oh, one more thing. The reason the position opened up is because the previous person in the job couldn't do it and was asked to leave the company. It's funny, actually; his background was very similar to yours. Welcome to management!"

This short story may sound a little over the top, but many people have been placed in this position. If you are a new manager or a soon-to-be manager, then good for you for buying this book, you did a smart thing. In fact, I suggest that after finishing my book you go out and buy other management books. As you become more intimate with management topics, you will find that each author's view and perspective of leadership and management is slightly different. Use these different points of view to help you define your own management style.

Over time and with years of experience, you will find that being a manager is not a destination, it's a journey. I, for example, have been managing people for well over twenty years, and my management style, ability to lead, and knowledge of management continues to grow and evolve.

When reading this chapter, consider the following questions:

- Are you sure you want to be a manager?
- If you are being promoted to manage the group where you are currently working, do you understand and do you feel comfortable with how the relationship with your current coworkers will change?
- Once in a management role, will you have to change how you dress or how you act? If so, do you feel comfortable with these changes?

Good luck with your management journey, enjoy the chapter and happy reading.

MAKE SURE YOU WANT TO BE A MANAGER

Most people go to school to learn a specific profession that interests them. Then, over time as they gain expertise, experience and an understanding of their profession and industry they are asked to do something totally different, manage people.

As a manager, you will still be involved in the work your department is doing, but it will be different. Instead of doing the work, you will be managing people and overseeing the work performed by your team. It is important that you understand that

- Managing is very different from doing
- You should make the conscience decision that you would rather be a manager than an individual contributor

Most of the topics in my weekly column have discussed your responsibilities as a manager. What I would like to emphasize here, is that one of your first responsibilities as a new manager is to transition your old responsibilities to a member of your team. If you try to continue doing your old job while learning and performing your new job, you will most likely fail at both. My one caveat to this statement is sometimes a manager's job is better described as "Player Coach", namely your job description includes a combination of supervisory and task related responsibilities. In this case, it is possible to be successful in both roles because you are being asked to do a little of each, not a full time job of each.

Over time, particularly if you are in a technical job, like computer programming or engineering, your technical skills will eventually become stale and out of date. This doesn't mean you can't lead the group. It means that without ongoing practice and training in new technology, you will not be able to sit down and personally perform the tasks being performed by your team.

If you truly enjoy hands-on work and don't have a strong interest in managing people, then moving into a management position may not be the right career move for you. I have seen a number of very talented technologists try management, not like it, and go back to an individual contributor role. Managers generally make more money than the individual contributors, so if you want to remain an individual contributor there is a cost, but there is also a cost to having a job that you don't enjoy.

My goal here is not to scare you away from becoming a manager, but rather to help assure that you are moving in the right direction that is right for you professionally. When deciding to move into management consider the following:

- Is being a manager something you will be happy doing?
- Do you need additional training to be the best manager you can be?
- Will you try to maintain your current technical skills?
- If you become the manager, what effect will it have on the relationship with your current co-workers and are you ok with that change?

Personally, I love being a manager. I find it to be challenging, creative, and rewarding. That said, I must say that there are also times that I find it to be frustrating and look fondly on the days of being an individual contributor. A friend of mine who has also been a manager likes to joke that management would be great if it wasn't for the people. For me, moving into the management ranks was a great move.

The primary advice and takeaways from today's column is to know that:

- Before becoming a manager make sure that a management job is right for you
- You'll find that as a manager, managing the work is very different than doing the work
- Being a manager can be great, if it's right for you

Until next time, manage well, manage smart, and continue to grow.

Congratulations, you get to manage your friends

Wow, the old manager left, and they had to pick a new one. You had more experience than most of the people in the group. You also do great work, are often asked for help by less-skilled team members, and are viewed as a team leader. As a result, you were promoted, and now you're the manager! First, the good news:

- You may get a nice bump up in pay
- Your friends and family will be proud of you
- You'll be taking on new and exciting responsibilities

Now the bad news:

- Your relationship with your coworker-friends will begin to change
- You will have to learn to delegate tasks to people that were previously your peers
- You may have to discipline your friends
- You will have to be much more careful as to what you say to your work-friends, remember, they are now your employees.

Generally speaking, you will find that the more junior people will be happy you got the job because they see that the company promotes from within, and they know they are not ready to be managers. Yet in a year or two, these same people will hope you leave so they can take your place. Others in your group may be jealous and/or resentful of you because they think they should have gotten the job instead of you. Others will be happy you got the job, because they think it will be good for their career. In other words, they think you like them, or at least that you like them more than the old boss did. There will also be others who could care less. These people have no desire to become managers; you're just a different guy in a suit who will most likely be gone in a year or two anyway.

In all cases, however, you are now the boss. They know that their next raise, promotion, and maybe paycheck are in your hands. They will be nicer to you, let you get coffee first at the coffee machine, and slowly start acting more like subordinates than peers. They will also be more guarded about what they say to you. After all, they can't complain to you about the boss anymore! You are the boss. In reality, you're no longer one of the gang. The best way to understand this phenomenon, the change from subordinate to manager, is to think about how you treat your boss and to understand that you are now being treated that way by your subordinates.

The primary advice and takeaway for today's column is to know that:

- As the new boss, your relationship with your work-friends will change
- This change must take place for you to become a successful manager
- You must embrace and help facilitate this change
- You should make this change at a speed that is comfortable for you
- Your goal here is not to loose your friends, it's to maintain your friendships, but modify them in a way that allows you to manage effectively while in the workplace.

For additional information on today's topic, I'd like to refer you to my book, _Manager Mechanics: Tips and Advice for First-Time Managers_. For comments on this topic or suggested future topics, please email me at eric@ManagerMechanics.com.

Until next time, manage well, manage smart, and continue to grow.

THE MANAGEMENT DRESS CODE

Dressing appropriately at work will not necessarily help you, but not following your company's unwritten dress code norms can hurt your upward mobility. Certainly there are general business rules that define what is and is not acceptable to wear in the workplace. Every company is different, so be careful when adapting this advice to your specific work environment.

As an individual contributor, you are primarily judged on how well you perform a specific task. If you are a computer programmer, you're judged on how well you program. If you are a telephone sales person, you're judged on how much you sell. As a manager, you are judged on your decision-making ability; this includes ALL types of judgment, including what you wear. After all, if you don't have the common sense to wear something appropriate to work, how can you be trusted to make good business decisions? This question may seem superficial, but within many organizations it's also very true.

Consider the following:

- If you are an individual contributor and would like to get promoted, observe how your manager and how his/her peers are dressed.
- If you are a new manger, observe how your peers are dressed.
- If you want to get promoted to the next management level, see how the level above you dresses.

As silly as this dress code stuff may sound, (Truth is, it originally sounded a little funny to me) it's true. For example, let's say that the first time you went to your boss' staff meeting you wore jeans and everyone else was wearing a suit and tie, how would you feel? You would most likely feel out of place. This would only have to happen to you once, and you would begin to pay more attention to how you and others dress.

As a personal example, early in my career I worked for a large computer manufacturing company. It was a great company, but no longer exists. The company had no company-wide dress code. That said, different parts of the company had unspoken rules of what to wear. If you were in sales or marketing, you wore a suit. If you were in finance, you dressed business casual. If you were in engineering or software development, you wore jeans and a cool looking tee-shirt. My job occasionally caused me to visit all three parts of the company. The only way all three organizations would take me seriously, was if I kept three sets of clothes in my car and changed what I was wearing as I drove from location to location. This was a little extreme, but it worked well.

The primary advice and takeaway for today's column is:

- As a manager, the dress code rules become a matter of showing good judgment
- What you wear to work may not necessarily help your career, but it can hurt it
- Appropriate work attire is different from company to company
- Different parts of your company may have different dress code customs
- Be cognizant of your company's unwritten dress code customs and dress accordingly.

For additional information on today's topic, I suggest the book _The Etiquette Advantage in Business_ by Peggy Post & Peter Post. For comments on this topic or suggested future topics, please email me at eric@ManagerMechanics.com.

Until next time, manage well, manage smart, and continue to grow.

WORKING WITH OTHER MANAGERS

Rule number one is to be a team player. It will make it easier for you, easier for your boss and easier for your group.

Assuming that your peers are also managers, your boss is then a manager of managers. As a result, his/her job is very different from yours. Whereas your job is to be sure that specific hands on work is being appropriately performed, your boss' job is to assemble a cohesive management team that works together as a unit for the greater good of the organization.

Unless you are very, very good or you are best friends with your boss, not being a team player will eventually cause you to be pushed out of the organization. Your boss wants a team that works together. Also, if your peers can't or won't work with you, they can make your life miserable. Also, never forget about reorganizations. If your boss leaves or is promoted, there is a large probability that you may find yourself working for one of your current peers. Now guess what, if you treated this person poorly when he/she was your peer, chances are he/she will be very unpleasant to you as your manager. Something thing to keep in mind is that helping your peers also helps your boss. As your manager wants you and your department to be successful, he/she also wants his/her other managers and their departments to be successful.

All that said, working with your peers is not always a bed of roses. Depending on your company's culture and/or your specific job function, you may find yourself continually competing with your peers for resources, budget dollars, control of specific business areas, bonus dollars, stock options and many other things. As a result:

- Learn the rules of the game
- Don't take advantage of your peers (too much)
- Don't be a push-over and let your peers take advantage of you

You will find that many of the rules you learned in elementary school still apply.

- If you let them take your lunch money today without a fight, they will probably try to take it again tomorrow
- If you are willing to take the blame for their issues today, you will probably be blamed for their problems tomorrow
- If you show leadership and initiative today, over time people may be willing to follow your lead
- If you don't play well in the sandbox, you won't be invited to play

Working with other managers is a different dynamic than working with other individual contributors. This primary difference is because you are managing the work, not doing the work. Thus, your role is more about coordination, communication and cooperation. As a manager, generally speaking, competence is assumed. Your success or failure in a particular role very often has very little to do with your personal skills and/or abilities. Your success has more to do with how your personality and working style fits into the organization's culture and your personal relationship with your boss and fellow managers.

The primary advice and takeaways from today's column is to know that:

- Be a team player, it can make life easier for you, your boss, your team, and your peers
- Your success as a manager at a particular company will be based more on how your personality and work-style gels with an organization rather than on your skills and/or abilities
- Office politics at the manager level are very different than at the individual contributor level

For additional information on today's topic, I suggest the following book _Secrets to Winning at Office Politics: How to Achieve Your Goals and Increase Your Influence at Work_ by Marie G. McIntyre.

Until next time, manage well, manage smart, and continue to grow.

SPAN OF CONTROL RULES

The term "Span of Control" refers to the number of direct reports a manager can personally manage effectively. The general rule of thumb is that a manager can effectively manage about seven people.

Seven people may not sound like a lot, but it is. When you consider that you have to oversee their work, mentor them, assure that each team member has enough to do, write annual (or semi-annual) performance reports, salary plans, bonus plans, deal with their professional and personal problems, and get your own work done, seven people is plenty.

I have seen departments where ten, fifteen or even twenty people are reporting to one manager. Many members of these groups felt neglected, underappreciated, see no opportunity for promotion, and in many cases, be under-utilized.

I'm not saying you should never manage more than seven people. I am saying that if your department has more than seven people, you should think about dividing your group into teams, or at least have part of your group report to a team leader, that reports to you. For example, if the accounting department has ten people, three working on General Ledger, three on Accounts Receivable and four on Accounts Payable, you could have the most appropriate person in each area be a team leader, thus giving you three rather then ten direct reports. This approach not only gives you more time to do your work, but it also provides a career path for the people in your group.

As the manager of a large or growing group, it can be very hard for you, and emotional for your group, to divide them into teams for the following reasons:

- All team members are currently reporting directly to you and may feel resentful that they are now reporting to fellow team member

- It may be hard for those you promoted to transition to a leadership role and now be managing their friends
- It may be hard for you to decide the best way to divide up your team
- You may not want to rock-the-boat by changing things and risk changing the group's internal dynamics
- You may feel personally threatened if there are junior managers in your department; one of them one day may take your job.

All of the above reasons are valid and appropriate. The issue is that if you don't eventually correct span of control problems, the following outcomes may occur.

- Your team members may begin to leave due to a lack of attention or promotional opportunities
- Your manager may reduce your responsibility by splitting your team into multiple groups and make you the manager over only one area
- Your manager may replace you and bring in a manager that can design a more effective and traditional organization structure

Span of control and organization design could fill a book, let alone a newspaper column. My goal here is just to get you thinking about the topic and to have a general understanding of industry thoughts and best practices.

The primary advice and takeaways from today's column is to know that:

- The general rule of thumb is that a manager can effectively manage about seven people
- If you have more than seven direct reports, consider breaking them into teams

- Not having a traditional reporting structure has the potential to cause issues for your group, your company, and yourself.

For additional information on today's topic, I suggest the following book *Levers Of Organization Design: How Managers Use Accountability Systems For Greater Performance And Commitment* by Robert Simons.

Until next time, manage well, manage smart, and continue to grow

CONSIDER YOUR NEXT MOVE

Now that you are a manager, what's next? If you have an answer to this question, then good for you. If you don't, then start planning. It has been documented again and again that people who carefully plan their career tend to be more successful professionally.

Now would be a good time to contact your mentor and/or professional career coach to plan out your short term and long term goals and plans. When planning your next steps, consider the following questions:

- Do you enjoy being a manager and do you wish to continue on a management path?
- Are you happy at your current company and industry?
- What opportunities exist at your current employer and do you believe you will be considered for these opportunities?
- Is an advanced degree, specific certification, or other credential needed for you to be promoted?
- Are there things that you could be doing as part of your current job to help position yourself for a promotion?

Another thing to consider when deciding your next professional move has nothing to do with your profession; it's your personal life. Remember, your job is just part of who you are and part of what you do. In order to be successful not only in work, but in life, you must consider your personal priorities also. That said, when considering your next move, also think about the following questions:

- What are your thoughts on work-life balance?
- Does your personal life allow you to travel for work? If yes, then how much?
- Do your family and personal obligations allow you to move to a different city, state, or country if the opportunity arises?

- Will you be happiest in a job that helps people, even if the pay is less?
- Would a job that does or does not have a 9:00 – 5:00 schedule be more suited to your lifestyle and personal situation?
- If you know you could not fail, what would you like your job to be?

These questions and others like them will help you define a next job that meets the combination of your personal and professional aspirations. That's the real win.

Another thing to consider is where do your talents lie? If you can find a job, in management or elsewhere, that takes advantage of your personal strengths and doesn't require strong abilities where you are not as capable, it will greatly enhance your chance of success.

Lastly, what are your interests? Using an old expression, "What floats your boat?" If you are going to be doing something five days a week, it might as well be something you are interested in.

Once you have an idea of your professional direction, your next steps will begin to become obvious. The sooner you figure out where you want to go, the sooner you can begin your journey in earnest.

The primary advice and takeaways from today's column is to know that:

- People who carefully plan their career tend to be more successful professionally
- Your job is only part of who you are and what you do. Consider your personal priorities also.
- When considering your next move be aware your interests, strengths and weaknesses, family obligations, and wanted work-life balance.

For additional information on today's topic, I suggest the book _The Truth About Managing Your Career_ by Karen Otazo.

Until next time, manage well, manage smart, and continue to grow.

MANAGEMENT STYLE

This chapter is somewhat unique from the other chapters of the book. Generally speaking, the other chapters discuss how things should be done and/or how to deal with people. This chapter looks inward rather than outward, and, in essence, raises a number of questions:

- What type of manager do you want to be?
- How do you want to treat those that work for you?
- Do you want help defining your management style or do you want to figure it out on your own?
- Do you want to be a manager, a leader, or both?

As you consider these questions, know that there are no right or wrong answers. The trick is for you to be true to yourself and make decisions that are right for you and consistent with your values, personality, strengths, weaknesses, and professional goals.

As time goes by and you grow as a person and a professional, you may find that the answers to these questions change. Somewhere down the line you may look back on your original answers and wish you had answered them differently. Change is inevitable, but don't think poorly about your past decisions; you can't change the past. That said, you should learn from your previous decisions and use your past experiences to continue to grow, both personally and professionally.

On a personal note, I, like most others, have said, "I wish I knew then what I know now." I personally rebut this train of thought by knowing I always did the best I could with the knowledge and experience I had at the time.

Enjoy the chapter and happy reading.

Defining your management style

What kind of manager do you want to become? Do you want to dig deeply into the details? Do you want to be a visionary that only gets involved at a high level? Do you want to drive your people as hard as possible? Do you want to make sure that your staff has a good work/life balance? Do you want your staff to like you, be afraid of you, hate you, respect you and/or want to be you? The answers to these questions will be partially based on your personal beliefs, abilities, temperament and values. Other answers will be based on your conscious decisions of how you want to manager.

There are many great books that discuss management practices and techniques. In general, these books recommend that you provide leadership, give direction, provide encouragement, delegate responsibility, give constructive criticism and continually communicate. You and you alone must decide if you want take the time and effort to learn from these books and which suggested techniques to personally employ.

Regarding which of these techniques to add to your personal repertoire, everyone has their own strengths and weaknesses. Therefore, some of the suggested management practices will be easier or harder for you to adopt. That said, through effort, I believe almost any person can employ almost any management technique if they put their mind to it.

Over time, you may see your management style evolve.

- You may start out very strict and overbearing and years later become mentoring and supportive.
- You may start out mentoring and supportive and end up strict and overbearing.
- You may quickly fall into a management style that is successful for you and maintain it through your entire career.

In any case, you will see that as you grow personally through your life, you will also gain a deeper understanding and a clearer perspective of what it takes to make a good manager and what type of manager you want to be.

As for me, I'm a very different manager now than I was twenty years ago, or even ten years ago. I have always tried to be fair, supportive, and mentoring. As time moved on and my personal and professional experience increased, I have found that I have become much more effective giving constructive criticism, setting department goals, thinking strategically, motivating my team and mentoring my staff.

As you work to formulate your personal management style, consider the following items which, in retrospect, I wish someone had told me early in my career.

- You need to find a style that is consistent with your personality. If you don't, you won't enjoy being a manager.
- If you treat your staff like you would like to be treated, you are probably on the right track.
- Learn by watching other managers. In fact, next week's column is all about watching and learning from other managers.
- Know that everyone makes mistakes. The trick is to learn from those mistakes and not make them again.
- Be open minded and willing to take advice from your boss, other managers, and even your staff.
- Know that defining your management style is an ongoing journey, not a destination.

Lastly, know that my goal here is not to push you to be a specific kind of manager, it is to help you grow into the type of manager you would like to be.

The primary advice and takeaways from today's column is to know that:

- Over time, you may see your management style evolve
- Be willing to take advice and learn from other managers

- All new managers make mistakes, the trick is to learn from them and not make them again
- Find a management style that is consistent with your personality.

For additional information on today's topic, I suggest the book _Understanding and Changing Your Management Style_ by Robert C. Benfari.

Until next time, manage well, manage smart, and continue to grow.

Leadership verses Management

There are various opinions on the difference between leadership and management. In fact, there have been a number of great books and professional articles written on the subject. My opinion can be very simply described.

- Leadership is proactive
- Management is reactive
- The best managers have a combination of both

A good manager reacts appropriately to management requests, business issues and business processes. By management requests, I am referring to special requests for analysis, cutting your budget as needed, and other similar activities. Example business issues include dealing with difficult employees, solving disputes with vendors, helping customers and generally handling unforeseen events. By business process, I am referring to properly following company and department level procedures. Company level processes include activities like budgeting, salary planning and performance reporting. Department level processes encompass the workflow oriented tasks needed to make a department effective and efficient.

The ability to effectively execute this management side of your job is essential to your success.

The concept of leadership is more of an intangible. Leadership is the ability to formulate vision and articulate that vision in such a way that other people understand it, embrace it and move toward its reality.

In a company setting, leaders are the agents of change, the internal entrepreneurs and the risk takers. As you can see, adding leadership to your management role adds an entirely new dimension to your job and to your value to the company.

Leadership in a corporate setting also reveals itself in another way, namely, through the respect, loyalty and trust of your staff. In its truest essence, leadership is the ability to take control and have people that wish to follow. In a corporate setting, effective leadership can be a catalyst that drives department productivity, product quality and organizational pride.

I should point out, that companies need all three types of managers, namely, management oriented, leadership oriented, and those with a combination of both management and leadership attributes.

What I have found is that

- Management-only type managers tend to drive processes and efficiencies
- Leadership-only type managers drive change and innovation
- Managers with both skill sets tend to do a little of both.

Over the years I have worked for all three types of there managers. I have also learned to respect all three types of these managers. They are all vital to health, strength and growth of companies of all sizes. It's interesting; I've seen the same manager be very successful in one company and unsuccessful in another company. In both companies this person worked just as hard, had similar responsibilities, and was in a similar organizational role. The difference between the two companies where he worked was the corporate culture. One company had a higher respect for managers that were innovative and leadership oriented and the other company primarily rewarded managers who followed existing process. Both were high quality companies, but they operated very differently.

From your perspective, I suggest you consider the following.

- Learn to work with all three types of managers and respect their different types of contribution to the company
- Decide which type of these managers you would like to be

- Understand the importance of your company's internal culture and how it relates to manager success. Then, make sure you are at a company that appreciates your personal style, strengths, and characteristics.

The primary advice and takeaways from today's column is to know that:

- The three primary manager styles are; management-only, leadership-only, and a combination of the two
- Decide what type of manager you would like to be
- Make sure you are at a company that rewards and respects your personal management style.

For additional information on today's topic, I suggest the book *Organizational Culture and Leadership* by Edgar H. Schein.

Until next time, manage well, manage smart, and continue to grow.

Throughout your career, you should try to learn from the managers around you. Watch them closely and see what they do right and wrong. By doing so, you can learn from their successes and failures and then adjust your management style accordingly. This includes your bosses, your peers and in time, the managers that report to you.

When observing fellow managers, here are some things to looks for:

- How does the manager treat his/her subordinates and how the subordinates react to it?
- How does the manager work with his peers to get things done and is he/she successful?
- What decision process does the manager use? In other words, does he look for consensus, analyze alternatives, go on gut feeling, take advice from others, act quickly, base decisions only on politics, and so on?
- What is the manager's work ethic?
- How is the manager viewed by his staff, peers and management?
- How does the manager act under pressure?
- How does he act and lead meetings?

When analyzing these managers, consider things from both the general and specific perspective.

- As an example of a general topic; does he/she treat his subordinates fairly and equally?
- As an example of a specific topic; what process and steps does he/she use to estimate his annual budget?

Just for the record, when I say to observe your fellow managers, I don't mean to follow them around; that would be creepy. I mean just pay attention to the way they work. Also, if appropriate, and if you feel comfortable doing so, ask them questions and use them as a mentor.

I have had the pleasure of working for some great managers over the years. Many of the principles I have discussed are based on what I learned by observing their management styles. In fact, while writing this column, one of my best managers comes to mind. He was a great manager and at the time I didn't even realize it. It was very early in my career, before I was a manager. He had a way of making everything a teaching moment. When I did things well, he not only told me I did, but explained why. Conversely, when I made mistakes he also let me know it, but explained why. There are certainly many other things that are required to be a good manager, but he had the mentoring thing down to a science.

I have also worked for managers that were overbearing, dishonest, obnoxious and just plain mean. I also learned from them. I learned what it feels like to be stuck working for a bad manager and made mental notes to never be like them.

I have also learned an enormous amount by watching managers over the years that were my peers. The trick to doing this effectively is being able to occasionally step away from the office politics and just view your peers as other people trying to do their best. Like you, there are some things they do well, and some things they don't do well but don't want anyone to know it.

The main message for you here is to learn by watching other managers and incorporate their positive attributes into your management style. Additionally, watch what other managers do wrong and learn from their mistakes.

The primary advice and takeaways from today's column is to know that:

- Watching and learning from your boss, peers and other managers can provide you with insights that can further your career
- You can learn from both great managers and bad managers, you just learn different things

Until next time, manage well, manage smart, and continue to grow.

FINDING A MENTOR

I can't overemphasize the advantage of having one or two knowledge-able, well connected mentors. A mentor is a person more senior than yourself who takes an interest in you and your career. It can be a

- Family member
- Friend of the family
- Old boss
- Professor you had in college
- Or anyone else

The key is that they can give you quality professional advice and ideally have the contacts and influence to help move you ahead professionally. The proper mentor can greatly accelerate your upward professional movement by connecting you to the right person or providing you with the insight to make the right decision,

There will be times during your career when you are at a professional crossroad when the help and advice of a mentor can be enormously valuable. Should you take the new job? Should you go back to school full time? Should you take a promotion even if it also means going to work for a person you don't trust or respect? Do you fire a poor performing employee if he is the president's nephew? The answers to questions like these can have a major impact (good or bad) on your career. Advice from a person more experienced than you can provide you with the insights to take the right step.

Your mentor should be someone you like, trust, and respect. It also should be someone that can give you good advice. You can get bad advice anywhere. Really good advice is hard to come by.

At times in my career I have been on both sides of the mentoring scenario. When I have had the good fortune to have someone of knowledge, experience, and position to take interest in me, it has been of incredible value to me. It's because of those experiences that I find myself always willing to help others when able to do so. In my mind, I'm paying it forward as a thank you to those who took an interest in me. If you have a mentor, consider the following.

- No relationship should be a one way street
- Treat your mentors in the way they deserve, with respect, trust, thankfulness and friendship
- Mentors help people out of the goodness of their heart and because they have taken an interest in your success
- They know that because of their position relative to yours that it will be difficult or impossible to reciprocate in kind
- Not being able to reciprocate in kind to a mentor is ok, it's the nature of mentoring
- As a thank you to your mentor, pay it forward and be willing to be a mentor when the situation presents itself

Lastly, as an additional piece of advice, don't just sit back and wait for a mentor to find you. If you know of someone you respect, trust, and you think could help you, reach out to that person in a respectful and appropriate way. At best, you have found yourself a mentor and potentially life-long friend and confidant. At worse, they say no, but may actually be flattered that you asked.

The primary advice and takeaways from today's column is to know that:

- The right mentor can be of great value to you both personally and professionally
- Mentoring is a two way street; treat your mentors with respect, trust, thankfulness and friendship
- Feel free to appropriately reach out to a potential mentor and ask for their assistance

For additional information on today's topic, I suggest the book _The Mentor Leader: Secrets to Building People and Teams That Win Consistently_ by Tony Dungy.

Until next time, manage well, manage smart, and continue to grow.

Work is not a democracy it's a dictatorship

You are not only the manager of your group, you're also its leader, primary advocate, mood setter, chief bottle washer, and of course its chief decision maker. That said, feel free to get input from your staff and/or other knowledgeable parties, but at the end of the day, the decision is yours and yours alone. In fact, if you try to be too nice and leave every decision to a department vote, you will be viewed as indecisive, weak, ineffective and an obstacle to getting things done. On a lighter note, the good news is that you get to call your department's shots. Cool!

Now that you know you're the one on the hook to be decisive, consider the following when making decisions.

- Be fair to your staff members and don't pick favorites.
- If appropriate, get input from your staff. It will give them a feeling of inclusion and make them feel more comfortable with the decisions you make.
- Be respectful of your staff members' feelings, professional aspirations, abilities, limitations, and general attitude.
- It's ok to leave fun decisions, such as the location of the holiday party, to team consensus.
- Make sure to do your due diligence on important decisions and document your findings. You'll make better decisions. It will add to your personal credibility and it will help protect you if the wrong decision was made.
- Only make decisions that are yours to make.

  - Making decisions that should only be made by your boss can get you in trouble.
  - Making decisions that should be made by your staff members usurps their authority, hurts team

morale, and reduces their ability to grow professionally.

In addition to all of the above, don't make a decision based on how it makes you feel. It's your job and obligation to make decisions based on what is best for your company, even if it's not always in your personal best interest. If you follow this advice, you may find that sometimes it takes real courage to do the right thing. This attitude is best summed up in the expression "Business is Business", and it's true. I once had to lay off a good friend; he understood it, but I hated it. Conversely, a friend of mine had to lay me off. Even though I agreed with her decision, she hated to do it. In both of these cases, the right decision was made.

A new manager once told me that he hated to make decisions because he was afraid of being wrong. I told him two things. First, not making a decision is a decision. It is a decision not to act. Second, if a decision needs to be made and you don't make it, someone else will. If that someone is a member of your staff, then sooner or later they may have your job and you will be looking for a new one.

The primary advice and takeaway for today's column is to know that:

- Only make decisions that are yours to make
- When making difficult decisions, do the appropriate due diligence and document your decision process
- If a decision needs to be made , make it, or someone else will

For additional information on today's topic, I suggest the following books _Smart Choices: A Practical Guide to Making Better Decisions_ by John S. Hammond, Ralph L. Keeney, and Howard Raiffa and _Winning Decisions: Getting It Right the First Time_ by J. Edward Russo and Paul J.H. Schoemaker. For comments on this topic or suggested future topics, please email me at eric@ManagerMechanics.com.

Until next time, manage well, manage smart, and continue to grow.

Following the company line

Rule number one. Sometimes you can complain about the company to your peers, but never complain about the company to your subordinates or superiors. Think about it, as a manager, are you going to promote someone who continually complains to you about the company? I think not. Now let's look at the other side of the coin. How motivated would you be if your boss was continually saying the company is lousy, doing poorly and is badly run? You may be motivated to update your resume and find a new job.

Remember, as a manager, you're part of the management team. This means the following:

- You're the voice of the company to those who report to you
- Your job is to assist senior management in meeting their objectives
- It's your responsibility to take senior management's vision and adapt it to your department
- You're a representative of your company to vendors, clients, government agencies, and the press
- If you don't follow company rules and/or work to support company goals, it will affect your raise, your bonus, your upward mobility and possibly your job

That said, if your company is doing something dishonest or illegal, it is a different matter, but you cannot ignore your company's new marketing plan or vacation policy because you would have personally designed them differently.

A number of years ago I reported to one of my favorite managers. When she made decisions I didn't like or agree with, she allowed me to raise my concerns. Sometimes she agreed with me and the decision was modified. Other times, she stayed with her original decision and I would work diligently to follow her instruction. This worked out well for both of us. I know I could safely present my concerns without fear of punishment and she knew that once a final decision was made, I would follow her direction regardless of my personal feelings. When working with your staff, I suggest that you treat your staff the way my boss treated me with openness and respect.

Other decisions may be made above your manager's level, thus making it very difficult or impossible for you to directly challenge or affect new company policies, procedures and/or initiatives. In these cases, consider the following:

- Follow the internal rules and procedures on company-wide hiring, performance review, budget planning and other processes. These systems can only work efficiently if everyone in the company does them the same way
- Support official company policies even if you don't personally like them or agree with them, it's your job as part of the management team
- Speaking poorly about your company to other employees may be viewed as very unprofessional, particularly by those who like or agree with the policy/procedure you are bad-mouthing

The primary advice and takeaway for today's column is to know that:

- Managers of all levels are part of the company management team and must work to help meet corporate goals and objectives
- As part of the management team you represent your company in all vendors, clients, government agencies and press interactions, so act accordingly in all circumstances
- You're the voice of the company to those who report to you. As a result, your interaction with your staff must be consistent with company policies, practices, and procedures.

Until next time, manage well, manage smart, and continue to grow.

ALLOWING FOR EMPLOYEE'S PERSONAL NEEDS

There is an old expression that says, "People should work-to-live not live-to-work." That said, upon occasion, and within certain bounds, you should allow an employee's personal life to take precedent over their job. The concept here is that if you have a good employee who is working through a difficult family, personal, or health issue you should help him or her out.

Assisting an employee at their time of need has the following benefits.

- As a human being, it feels really good to be able to really help someone.
- It builds incredible loyalty from the employee toward you and the company
- It may save a good employee from leaving your firm to care for the issue
- People talk. The other members of your team will know you did something to help a team member. This in turn will increase the team's loyalty to you.
- At a future time, when extra time or effort is needed to meet a deadline, your team will be there for you because you were there for them.

Over the years I have occasionally had a team member ask me for help. One person asked if she could take two-hour lunches for a couple of months until she found new long term care for her elderly mother. Due to her mother's health issues, her current facility could no longer meet her heeds. In additional to dealing with the emotions relating to her mother's declining health, it also caused major logistical problems for the employee. She said she would make up the time by coming in early. Not only did she come in early every day, but she often stayed late just to make sure that all her work was completed. I didn't keep a close watch of her coming and going because I trusted her. The best I could tell, she worked about two hours for every one hour she was out.

As they say, "No good turn goes unpunished". Therefore, when helping a member of your team in this way, consider the following.

- Talk to your manager and Human Resources (HR) first to make sure that you are acting in a way that is consistent with company policy
- Make sure this is viewed as a one-of-a-kind event, not as an ongoing favor
- Make it clear that this is for a specified length of time, with a specific end-date
- Be careful that you are not setting a department or company precedent
- You don't want to be seen as playing favorites or bending company rules
- If an employee asks "Why won't you do this for me, you did it for Larry?", you will have to answer it honestly and with valid reasoning.

The primary advice and takeaway for today's column is to know that:

- Assisting an employee dealing with a major personal issue is the right thing to do as a human being and can build long term employee loyalty
- Make sure to get management and HR approval before moving forward
- Make sure this is viewed as a one-time event with a specific end date

For additional information on today's topic, ask your HR department if your company has an Employee Assistance Program (EAP).

Until next time, manage well, manage smart, and continue to grow.

When an employee gives notice

When an employee gives notice, it's not in itself a good thing or a bad thing for you as the manager. It is, however, a reason for personal reflection as to why the person left. It's been my experience that employees leave companies for one of the following reasons.

1. Personal in nature and having nothing to do with their manager, the job, or the company
2. Professional in nature, but based on a personal decision
3. Getting off the ship before it sinks
4. Incompatibility with company culture, policies, and/or strategic direction
5. Professional and/or salary growth seems unattainable or far off at current employer
6. Lack of challenging work and/or skill set enhancement
7. Incompatibility with their manager

For this discussion, because it's a management advice column, let's consolidate the above list into three reasons:

- Things that have nothing to do with you
- Things that have a little to do with you
- Things that have a lot to do with you

Numbers 1 and 2 have nothing to do with you. The person may simply be following a love interest to another city, going back to school, switching profession, or other personal reasons. The best managers cannot and most likely will not try to stop the employee from leaving. They will wish the person well, if appropriate, offer to be a reference, and part on good terms.

Numbers 3, 4, and 5 are mostly related to your company, but you as their manager, are their most important company representative. You have the opportunity and responsibility to discuss company related issues with your employees. Without this manager-employee interaction, regardless of the professional level, most employees during times of uncertainty will fear the worst and act on those feelings.

Numbers 6 is related to both you and the company. Truth be told, your department may not be given anything truly interesting to work on. That said, as the department manager, if you think there are new and interesting things your department could be doing to help the company, it may be worthwhile to talk with your boss. If he/she agrees, it can provide an interesting project for your team; if he/she disagrees, at least you know you tried.

Also on Number 6, as the manager, there may be things that you can do within your responsibility to help challenge your team and help them grow professionally. These things could be

- Cross-training – allowing team members to gain new skills
- Delegation – Allowing team members to take on higher level tasks you have been doing
- Training – Formal training, if budget allows, and/or on-the-job training on higher-end skills, if appropriate, given your department goals
- Mentoring – Work with your team personally to help expand their skills

Number 7 is simply about the relationship that you have with the employee. You and the employee may just be very different people with very different personality types. Both are good, just different. In other cases, however,

- Your management style may be uncomfortable for the employee
- The employee may not agree with your assessment of his/her performance
- The employee may not feel they are being treated fairly by you
- Other manager/employee related issues

If you feel that the employee left for number 6 or 7, I am by no means suggesting you are at fault. That said, whenever a person working for me left, I always used it as a reason for personal reflection to fine tune my management style and grow as a person and a professional.

The primary advice and takeaways from today's column is to know that:

- Employees leave companies for many reasons; some reasons are related to their manager and some are not
- When an employee gives notice, use it as an occasion for personal reflection as how to grow as a manager and as a person

Until next time, manage well, manage smart, and continue to grow.

TEAM LEADERSHIP

One of the most important things you can do as a manager is properly lead your team.

As an individual contributor, you only managed yourself. Sure, your boss weighed in, but each of us is primarily and ultimately responsible for our own productivity, effectiveness, morale, and work quality. At this level, if you don't manage yourself correctly—and, as a result, have low productivity, work quality, and/or other issues—then you reduce the company's overall productivity on the scale of one person.

As a manager, however, your performance is multiplied across your entire team. If you have ten people on your team and you manage them well, your actions increase productivity by ten people. Conversely, if you manage your team poorly, then your actions reduce the productivity of ten company employees, which can jeopardize an entire company project or business function. This is the essence of why quality management is of the utmost importance in any company, regardless of its size, industry, or business function.

As such, the columns in this chapter are designed to help you manage your team as effectively as possible.

As you read, try to think about how the information can help you maximize your team's efficiency, productivity, and general morale. Additionally, ask yourself the following questions:

- Are your actions building or eroding the trust between you and your staff?

- Are your actions building or eroding the trust between your staff and the company?
- Are your actions enhancing or detracting from your staff's motivation, morale, and work quality?
- Are you training your staff in such a way that they can one day do *your* job?
- Do those in your team on a daily basis know their short-term and long-term objectives?

Asking yourself questions such as these can help your team's overall effectiveness and help you become the best manager you can be.

Enjoy the chapter and happy reading.

Developing trust

To be an effective manager, your team doesn't have to like you, they don't even really have to like working for you, but they do have to trust you. Otherwise, they will spend more time trying to protect themselves from you, rather than using their creative energies to follow your instructions. In short, you must be able to trust your group and they must be able to trust you.

Trust is an interesting thing between a subordinate and a manager. The manager has to take the lead and should consider doing the following.

- Demand honesty from your staff
- Make your anger known if someone lies to you or only tells you half truths
- Require that important information (good and bad) is communicated promptly
- Show your disapproval if someone only tells you the good news and not the bad news

Then, in return for their promptness and honestly, you should:

- Be honest to your staff members, if they feel they are being lied to, they will return it in kind.
- When your staff members tell you bad news and/or unpleasant information, you must work with them constructively to solve the problem, rather then punish them for it.
- Give appropriate praise and positive reinforcement when they act in an honest and appropriate manner.

All that said, you will find that your constructive and helpful attitude toward your team's problems will help you gain their trust. Additionally, they will also be more willingly to accept your advice, direction, and constructive criticism.

A friend of mine likes to say "Management would be great if it wasn't for the people". In that vein, if someone in your group is untrustworthy toward you, consider the following:

- Are they acting in an untruthful way because they don't trust you?
- If they don't trust you, do some sole-searching and try to figure out why. Remember, you are the manager; as a result, a trusted relationship begins with you.
- Next, try to correct the issue, thus forming a trusted relationship
- Lastly, if the person is just truly untrustworthy by nature, consider removing them from your group when the opportunity arises.

On a personal note, over the years I have worked for managers I trusted and a few managers that I learned not to trust. When working for managers I trusted, I found myself to be more creative, more energized, more committed to my work, more willing to take on business-appropriate risks, more productive, and more satisfied with my job. Now as the manager, wouldn't you want all of your people to feel this way? I would assume so.

The primary advice and takeaway for today's column is to know that:

- As the manager, the level of trust formed within your department starts with you
- Act in a way that help facilitate a trusting environment
- Your team will be more productive and effective if they trust you
- Trust in the workplace should be a two way street

For additional information on today's topic, I suggest the following books _Trust & Betrayal in the Workplace_ by Dennis S. Reina and Michelle L. Reina and _The SPEED of Trust_ by Stephen M.R. Covey. For comments on this topic or suggested future topics, please email me at eric@ManagerMechanics.com.

Until next time, manage well, manage smart, and continue to grow.

MOTIVATING YOUR GROUP

Management in the truest sense of the word is the ability to get things done through the efforts of other people. Additionally, people do their best work when they are properly motivated. The thing you have to figure out as a manager is how to motivate your team.

From my perspective, motivating people has two main components; environmental and individual. Your job as the manager is to foster both of these components.

- **Environmental motivation** is best defined as the mood, sense of purpose, stability and dynamics of the group. In other words, "Is it a nice place to work?"
- **Individual motivation** refers to the things that motivate a specific person.

Regarding environmental motivation, to the extent possible

- Keep your team engaged with meaningful work
- Communicate, people like to be in the loop
- Foster a friendly and supportive atmosphere
- Provide opportunities for professional growth
- Bring meaning and importance to your team's work
- Help facilitate friendship between staff members
- Encourage teamwork
- Show appreciation to each member of your team for their individual and group accomplishments
- Where appropriate, include your staff members in the decision making process
- Publicly recognize individual employee accomplishments

One thing about environmental motivation is that as the manager of a single department; you are by definition part of a larger organization. As a result, no matter how good a manager you are, you can't totally control your group's environment.

Things such as company mergers, the company's financial stability and unreasonable goals and deadlines imposed on you by upper management can impose incredible stress on your department. Over time, it is inevitable that you will occasionally be placed in some of these difficult situations. Your ability to maintain and motivate your team during these tough times could very possibly be the difference between you getting promoted and being replaced.

Regarding individual motivation, the difficulty is that people are motivated by different things.

- The chance of promotion
- Professional recognition
- Opportunity to learn new things
- Feeling part of a team, particularly a winning team
- Money
- Challenging work
- Sense of purpose in their work, such as helping others
- Or sometimes, well, nothing at all.

Your job, as the manager, is to figure out what motivates each of your team members, and within the bounds of fairness, company policy, and appropriateness, provide them with these motivations.

The primary advice and takeaway for today's column is to know that:

- Motivating your staff to be productive and successful in turn helps you
- Create a general environment that is conducive to motivation
- Maintaining team morale and motivation during difficult company times is extremely hard, yet particularly important
- You have to work with each team member to assure that his or her individual needs are being met
- The key here is to meet each person's needs in a way that also meets your objectives and the objectives of the company.

For additional information on today's topic, I suggest the following book _Make the Right Choice: Creating a Positive, Innovative and Productive Work Life_ by Joel Zeff.

For comments on this topic or suggested future topics, please email me at eric@ManagerMechanics.com.

Until next time, manage well, manage smart, and continue to grow.

BUILDING LOYALTY

There is an old expression that says "To have a good friend you have to be a good friend." I believe that loyalty follows the same paradigm. As a manager, if you want your team to be loyal to you, then you have to be loyal to them. Furthermore, because you are the manager, your actions and attitudes will be the primary determining factor as to the cohesiveness and loyalty of your team members toward each other and toward you.

That said, the following items will help you build a loyal organization.

- Let your team members take credit for their accomplishments
- Protect them when problems and/or bad politics arise
- Go to bat for them when they need it
- You have to be a good mentor, good teacher and good listener
- Trust their judgment within the bounds of their authority
- Reward teamwork among your team members
- Help your team members move toward their personal and professional goals

There are also things that you should not do because it can dramatically undermine your efforts toward building loyalty. They are:

- Don't assume that your team will be loyal to you just because you are the manager, you must earn their loyalty through your attitudes and actions
- Don't take your teams loyalty for granted, continue to foster it
- Don't take advantage of your team's loyalty for your personal gain, once found out, their feelings toward you will we substantially diminished

People's loyalty is hard to achieve and once lost, very hard to reestablish. To illustrate this concept, consider the following story. In

Boston there are two main train stations, South Station and North Station. Joe lives south of Boston and commutes to his Boston-based job via South Station. Bill lives north of the city and takes the morning train into North Station. Each morning, for years, Joe and Bill walk past each other on their way to their respective offices. As time passes they begin to recognize each other and start saying hello as they pass. They even stopped once and had coffee together. Then, one morning Joe was in a very bad mood and when Bill said hello to Joe, Joe reacted by knocking Bill to the ground. Joe felt terrible about it, helped Bill up and apologized again and again. Bill forgave Joe, but never quite looked at him the same way again and was always a little more guarded when he and Joe passed.

As you would expect, the moral of this story is that as the manager you can't choose when to be loyal to your staff and when not to be. Building and maintaining a loyalty-based work environment, not only requires specific intention, but also requires ongoing consistency.

The primary advice and takeaway for today's column is to know that:

- If you want your team to be loyal to you, then you have to be loyal to them
- Your actions will determine the loyalty of your team members toward each other and toward you
- Don't take you teams loyalty for granted, continue to foster it
- Once lost, loyalty is hard or impossible to reestablish

For additional information on today's topic, I suggest the book _Loyalty Rules: How Today's Leaders Build Lasting Relationships_ by Frederick F. Reichheld.

Until next time, manage well, manage smart, and continue to grow.

Employee training, who needs what

It's been my experience that most companies agree that training is an important component of workforce productivity, talent management, employee morale and company competitiveness. The questions arise over what type of training to provide, who gets it and how much company time and money can be used to procure it. There is an old joke that training is both an employee right and a privilege. The employee generally thinks it's his right. His/her manager generally thinks that it's a privilege.

From a budget perspective training is generally categorized into two types

- Tuition reimbursement
- Department training budget

Tuition reimbursement is when the company pays for accredited college courses taken at night. In general, tuition reimbursement is considered (and budgeted) an employee benefit, like life insurance, and its budget is not usually reduced midyear. **Department training budget** is generally not for college credit and is designed to teach a specific hard or soft skill.

- **Hard skill** based class teaches a specific skill, like programming in Java or fixing a new type of refrigeration unit.
- **Soft skill** based training teaches things like time management, stress reduction, public speaking, and things of that type.

Going to user conferences, generally fall under the "Soft Skill" umbrella even though that is not always accurate and/or fair. A hard skill related class is usually easier to justify from a budget perspective if the class is needed to train an employee for an upcoming project because it gives the company a more tangible payback.

Generally, when companies go though their annual budget planning process, they usually include money for employee training. Training dollars are usually budgeted on a "per head" basis. In other words, during the budget process you will be told that each person in the company should be allocated a specified amount of training dollars, for example $1,000 a person. Therefore, if you have five people in your group, you will have a $5,000 training budget.

If the company does well that year, the training money stays in the budget. If the company does worse than expected, unfortunately one of the first things to be cut is usually training because it is a discretionary expense. This doesn't mean that companies feel that training is unimportant; it just means that it is an easy way to reduce short-term expenses. That said; if training is important to you and your group, send them to class early in the year while the dollars are still available.

Consider the question of who receives training, who goes to the trade shows, and so on. There is no generic answer for this, only a guideline, namely, be fair to your staff members but do what's right for the company. Additionally, be objective to the needs of the individuals in your group, assess the skill shortfalls within your department and do what's right. That said, you should always find a way to provide at least some training for everyone.

Lastly, remember to find the time and budget to take a training class yourself. Just because you're now a manager, it doesn't mean you should stop taking classes.

The primary advice and takeaways from today's column is to know that:

- Two primary ways to fund staff training are tuition reimbursement and department training budget
- There are two major types of training; hard skills and soft skills

- If possible, use your training budget early in the year in case budgets are cut
- Be fair regarding who gets training
- Always provide training in a way that meets company goals

For additional information on today's topic, I suggest the book _Getting Your Money's Worth from Training and Development: A Guide to Breakthrough Learning for Managers and Participants_ by Andrew McK. Jefferson, Roy V. H. Pollock, and Calhoun W. Wick.

Until next time, manage well, manage smart, and continue to grow.

Management by Objective (MBOs)

Another name for MBOs could be "stuff I promise to do next year" or "things I have to do if I want my bonus", but MBO sounds much more professional. Not all companies use MBOs, but I wanted to write on this topic because if your current employer is not using them, you may see them in the future.

While performance reviews primarily look at the year that just ended, MBOs look at the year ahead. At the manager level, MBOs generally contain a combination of department goals and personal goals. Examples of department goals include things such as

- Reduce bill processing time to five days
- Implement a new accounting system

Examples of personal goals include things such as

- Take a time management class (if you have the time :)
- Visit the Boston and San Diego offices

Then, at the end of the year, or at bonus time based on your companies schedule, your MBOs will be reviewed by your boss and he/she will make a determination as to whether or not you met your objectives.

One thing to consider when using MBOs, if the business environment changes during the year, your objectives will not be met and it's not your fault. For example, say you have an MBO to visit the Boston office and the office closes, you obviously can't go there. Thus, you should not be penalized for not going to Boston. (By the way, if you go to Boston have dinner in the North End, the Italian food is incredibly good.)

Departments are generally either process-oriented or project-oriented.

- **Process-oriented departments** have some discreet projects, but primarily perform the same set of tasks all year.

For example, the payroll department spends its whole year processing payroll.

- **Project-oriented departments**, like software development groups, have some process based tasks, but primarily spend their time on software projects.

MBOs in process-oriented departments tend to hold their relevance through the year, because, for the most part, their MBOs will be process-improvement based. MBOs in project oriented departments tend to loose their relevance, because business decisions are often made that dramatically change the list of projects. For example, if a software development manager has an MBO to build a Human Resources System and the new VP of Human Resources decides he/she likes the old system, the new system will never be built. Thus, the MBO to build the new Human Resources System is now irrelevant.

I personally have always been in favor of the MBO process. I believe that it has value for the company, individual departments, department managers and individual contributors for the following reasons

- The MBO process requires up front planning and forward thinking
- If done correctly, company goals, department goals, and individual goals are all aligned
- Each person in the organization knows their goals for the year ahead.
- At year end, each person can be measured against the goals they agreed to at year's start
- Individual MBOs can be the justification to receive needed training and work assignments

As one final piece of advice, make sure that your MBOs are consistent with your boss' MBOs and your subordinate's MBOs. If they are, your MBOs will be a lot easier to make.

The primary advice and takeaways from today's column is to know that:

- MBOs combine company planning with employee performance reviews
- MBOs at all levels (president to individual workers) should be aligned
- MBOs can provide you with your work roadmap for the year ahead
- MBOs can assist you in getting needed/wanted training and experience

Until next time, manage well, manage smart, and continue to grow.

Succession planning

If your boss came to you today and told you to start making plans for your replacement, you would probably think it's a bad thing. Well, in some cases it might be a bad thing. Then again, if your company is in the process of creating a company-wide succession plan, it's actually a good thing.

A succession plan can best be described as the activity of identifying people within the company that can potentially fill key positions if the current incumbent in the role is promoted, changes jobs or leaves the firm.

Believe it or not, your participation in the success of the planning process is a good thing for a number of reasons.

- Your boss will also be planning for his/her replacement, and it may be you
- If you can't be replaced, then you can't be promoted
- Participation in management level planning activities can be good for your career
- If you are selected as a potential replacement for someone more senior, you may be given training toward filling that future position

Regarding finding your own replacement, the truth is that if the company wants to replace you, they're going to do it with or without a formal succession plan. That said, the only truly bad thing about succession planning is it doesn't feel good to discuss your potential replacement with your boss. My answer to you, get over it. If the company, to its credit, has decided to do a company-wide succession plan you should participate honestly and enthusiastically.

At a personal level, I was actually promoted once because of a succession plan. Interestingly, it wasn't into my boss's job. I was promoted into a different department reporting to a person I barely knew. He knew that one of his managers would be leaving soon and needed to be replaced. Serendipitously, the company was in the process of creating a company-wide succession plan. He saw me present a topic unrelated to his department and was impressed. Then, with the assistance of Human Resources, he identified me as the person's replacement. The person left and I was promoted.

Now let's talk about succession planning as a corporate activity, rather than how it affects you personally. If done correctly, a quality succession plan gives management the information needed to effectively restructure, grow, and/or shrink the company as needed. It also provides insight into how to promote, reassign, and/or replace key company employees. For example, a company may need five managers to staff a new company division. The succession plan will help senior management decide how to back fill the people being moved.

As a simpler example, a manager accepts a position at another company and needs to be replaced. The succession plan provides a starting point in the replacement process.

Very often, succession planning is an activity that is included as part of an overall talent management program. Talent management is one of those terms that can be described in many ways. I like to think of it as the process of maximizing a company's bench strength by identifying, retaining, and developing key employees to meet future business opportunities and challenges.

The primary advice and takeaways from today's column is to know that:

- If done right, succession planning can be of great company value
- Participation in the succession planning process can help your career
- Who knows, you may be identified as your boss's future replacement

For additional information on today's topic, I suggest the book _The Executive Guide to High-Impact Talent Management_ by David DeLong and Steve Trautman. This book explains and illustrates the importance of talent management from an executive's perspective. If you are currently a senior executive or would one day like to be one, it's a great read.

Until next time, manage well, manage smart, and continue to grow.

DIFFICULT EMPLOYEES

Difficult employees are every manager's nightmare. They can hurt your team's overall productivity. They can hurt the overall atmosphere of the workplace. They can adversely affect fellow staff members, and they can hurt your department's and company's overall goals. Additionally, they can waste a disproportionate amount of your time, distracting your focus from other important business matters, reducing the amount of time you can spend with your other staff members, and generally driving you crazy.

The columns in this chapter are designed to help you deal with difficult employees from the following two perspectives:

- Using constructive criticism to empower employees to help themselves
- Defining the specific employee issue and then trying to deal with that issue in a customary way

Constructive criticism, if done right, can be of great value to both you and the person receiving it. It is of value to you, as the manager, because you are able to correct an employee-related issue in a non-confrontational manner. And it benefits the person receiving the criticism by opening a door to personal improvement.

On a personal note, I like receiving constructive criticism. I find that it helps me learn more about myself, my skills, and how I am viewed by others. It also helps me better perform tasks in a way that are of value to others. Truth be told, I find constructive criticism valuable not only in the workplace but also on the home front and life in general. My suggestion to you is to take the same approach.

As for defining an employee's specific issue and then working to correct it, you will see that I have some fun assigning names to various issues, but the advice is quite serious. Very often in my career I've had a staff member that did many things right but had one issue that seemed to overpower his/her otherwise good work. I have found that if I address the issue properly, I can turn a problem employee into a quality performer. In some cases, this turnaround has been almost immediate. People often simply aren't aware that they're doing something problematic, and are eager to adjust once they become aware.

The questions to ask yourself when reading this chapter are:

- Is there any constructive criticism that you could provide to members of your team that could help their performance and/or professional or personal growth?
- Do you have employees that fall into any of the seven categories described in this chapter? If yes, how can you effectively deal with them?
- Are there other categories that you would like to define? If yes, what corrective actions would you pursue?

Employee issues tend not to correct themselves unless the employee decides to leave. So the sooner you effectively address these issues, the sooner the problem will be solved. In the long run, this is good for your company, good for you, good for your department, and, more often than not, good for the employee in question.

Enjoy the chapter and happy reading.

Giving constructive criticism

Like a parent disciplining a child, the punishment must match the crime. You can't just fire someone just because you want to. If an employee makes a minor mistake or inadvertently breaks a company policy, it simply becomes a teaching moment. That said, if someone does something dangerous, illegal, or totally contrary to company policy you must act clearly, decisively, and quickly.

There are many different types of employee discipline. In future columns I'll deal with more severe forms of employee discipline, such as written warnings and termination. For now, let's just discuss a gentle but very effective form of discipline, constructive criticism, which is also often referred to as constructive feedback.

It has been my experience that sometimes you have a good employee doing the wrong thing. It may be due to a lack of skill in a particular area or it may be a lack of understanding of the rules. In either case, it's your job as the manager to take the person aside and explain what he/she is doing wrong and explain what is needed to improve/correct the situation. This is constructive criticism.

When giving constructive criticism consider the following steps:

1. Start by talking about something that the employee is doing well
2. Say that, in general, he/she is doing good work, but needs a little help in one particular area
3. Talk about the issue in a friendly, mentoring, and teaching type manner
4. Discuss specific steps that will help correct the issue
5. Discuss a date and/or time to have a follow up discussion on the topic
6. Change the subject to something fun and non-work oriented, like a local sports team or fun weekend plans

The order of these steps is designed to:

- Make the employee initially feel safe and thus not defensive.
- Be sure the employee understands that the issue
- Define action items and establish a timeframe for the issue correction
- Leave the employee with a positive feeling and willing to accept the needed feedback and follow through on the defined action plan

When I think back on my career in regard to constructive criticism, a memory comes to mind when I was the receiver of this type of advice. Early in my career I often did a very poor job proofreading my presentations. My manager at the time, who I still have great respect for, took me aside, explained the importance of proofreading and helped me develop a process to correct the issue. At the end of our conversation, I felt thankful for his help, but I also understood that it was a correction I was required to make quickly.

You should also remember that there may be times when you are the receiver of constructive criticism. That said, consider the following:

- Always welcome constructive criticism, even if you don't like to hear it, or like the person delivering it, it may be quality advice
- Feel free to solicit constructive criticism from those you trust, it may provide you with some insights on how other people perceive you

The primary advice and takeaway for today's column is to know that:

- Constructive criticism is an effective and gentle way for a manager to simultaneously give advice and correct an issue with an employee
- If done correctly, constructive criticism gives the employee three messages; advice on corrective action, support of the employee, and the need to change

For additional information on today's topic, I suggest the book *Job Feedback: Giving, Seeking, and Using Feedback for Performance Improvement* by Manuel London.

Until next time, manage well, manage smart, and continue to grow.

THE SEVEN TYPES OF DIFFICULT EMPLOYEES
– PART 1 OF 3

Let's say it like it is. Managing difficult employees isn't any fun. It wastes lots of time, takes lots of energy, and usually creates lots of paperwork. Now for the good news, well sorry, there is no good news. The best news I can give you is that if you handle the situation correctly you may be able to dramatically improve their attitude, work quality and general performance.

Now let's discuss what to do if you do have a difficult person on your team. To that end, I like to categorize difficult employees into the following seven categories:

- Sleazy
- Grumpy
- Lazy
- Brainy
- Tardy
- Dummy
- Troubled

Ok, I know this is a little corny, but this was more fun than categorizing them as types 1 to 7. Please note that the first five types are honesty and/or motivation based, the last two, could be you or I at any given time. In this week's column, I discuss the first two types, Sleazy and Grumpy. The other five types will be described in the future columns.

Sleazy: This type of person is marginally honest. He does not do anything blatantly illegal or clearly against company policy, but pushes the limits with no particular regard to the company, his fellow employees or your customers. Classic example activities of this kind of person includes

- Padding his expense account

- Selling inappropriate products to your customers
- Stealing customers and leads from other sales people
- Taking credit for other people's work
- Generally doing things that other employees find repugnant

Generally speaking, I don't trust this kind of person. My advice to you is not to trust them either and be pleasantly surprised if you find them to be honest. Your best plan of action to straighten them out is to

- Talk to your HR person first
- Then sit down with the employee (maybe with HR)
- Lay out the law in writing

As an example, if they have been selling inappropriate products to your customers, inform them that you will be monitoring their sales. Continue to say that if the practice continues, they will be reassigned or asked to leave the company. You have to be tough and make it plain to your group that questionable business practices are not acceptable.

Grumpy: Well, we all know grumpy people. You see it in their

- Facial expressions
- Speech
- Body language
- General attitude

There are a number of reasons why people are grumpy at work, some are personality related, some are non-work related and some are work related. From a personality perspective, these people are few and far between, but some people are just grumpy by nature. You have to learn to manage around their grumpiness, or over time, move them out of your department.

Non-work related grumpiness will be discussed in a future section.

Work related grumpiness can very often be corrected through good management (yes, your good management). Very often people are grumpy at work for a specific reason. These reasons include

- Low pay
- Lack of challenging work
- Lack of training
- Lack of visibility to upper management
- No perceived chance of advancement
- Other similar issues.

Your job as the person's manager is to work with the employee to define the specific issue or issues causing their unhappiness and define a plan to correct it. I have seen many peoples' attitudes improve dramatically when the proper steps are taken to address their concerns.

The primary advice and takeaways from today's column is to know that:

- There is potential to dramatically improve the attitude, work quality and general performance of difficult employees
- Try to categorize the specific difficulty and address that difficulty directly

For additional information on today's topic, I suggest the book _101 Tough Conversations to Have with Employees_ by Paul Falcone.

Until next time, manage well, manage smart, and continue to grow.

The Seven types of difficult employees
– Part 2 of 3

In last week's column, I introduced the concept of dealing with difficult employees by first classifying their specific difficulty and then taking specific action based on their classification. The seven were named Sleazy, Grumpy, Lazy, Brainy, Tardy, Dummy, and Troubled. As part of last week's column we discussed the issues and solutions for Sleazy and Grumpy. This week I'll be discussing Lazy, Brainy, and Tardy.

Lazy: This is the *"I'm going to do as little as possible to still keep my job"* guy. On a personal note, I'm a very hard worker, so lazy people drive me crazy. I personally have no tolerance for laziness, so I tend to continually be on these people to get their job done. One of the best ways to handle lazy people is to give them tasks that can be specifically measured in regard to quality and quantity. This approach allows you to

- Benchmark their current volume of work
- Objectively evaluate their increase or decrease in work output
- Take appropriate positive and negative actions as needed

Brainy: By brainy, I mean a "know-it-all". These people are typically hard working, smart and do a good job. This is a good thing. The problem is that they can drive their peers crazy and cause tension within the department. This problem can generally be fixed using the following steps

1. Occasionally have an honest discussion with the person
2. Ask him/her to quiet down a little bit
3. Ask him/her to treat fellow employees with more tolerance and respect

As a quick story, I once had a know-it-all type person working for me. The interesting thing was he did seem to know it all. He was a brilliant computer programmer. The problem was he wanted everyone to know it. To solve the problem I did two things. First, I talked with him about how to properly mentor less knowledgeable programmers. Second, I modified his role to include mentoring-type activities. Because of the mentoring lesson, the staff found him to be helpful, rather than boastful. Because of the job change, he was able to provide real value to the members of my team and the department in general. He also loved his new role and worked hard to enhance his mentoring skills.

Tardy: On occasion, everyone comes in late, has a long lunch or leaves early. But every so often, someone abuses the privilege. They seem to

- Always come in fifteen or twenty minutes late
- Continually take two hour lunches
- Always be leaving early

Not only are you not getting your money's worth from this person, but their lack of respect in the company's schedule can have a very disruptive effect to the rest of your team, particularly if your other team members are working long hours. I generally try to correct this problem by

- Having a discussion with the person
- Telling the person that his/her actions are unacceptable
- That he/she must work the required hours

If his schedule doesn't improve, then work with Human Resources (HR) to write a formal reprimand. This reprimand should include the specific actions to be stopped and the consequences if their actions continue. Generally, you will find that HR is very skilled in writing these types of letters.

The primary advice and takeaways from today's column is to know that:

- With lazy employees, assign work that can be measured in regard to quality and quantity
- With brainy employees, have occasional discussions with them to ease their overbearing manner
- With tardy employees, have a discussion and state the importance and your insistence on working the appropriate hours

Until next time, manage well, manage smart, and continue to grow.

For additional information on today's topic, I suggest the book _The Complete Idiot's Guide To Dealing With Difficult Employees_ by Robert Bacal.

THE SEVEN TYPES OF DIFFICULT EMPLOYEES
– PART 3 OF 3

In the last two columns, I introduced the concept of dealing with difficult employees by first classifying their specific difficulty and then taking specific action based on their classification. The seven types were named Sleazy, Grumpy, Lazy, Brainy, Tardy, Dummy, and Troubled. This week's column will discussed the issues and solutions for the last two difficult employee types; Dummy and Troubled.

Whereas the first five employee types are honesty and/or motivation based, the interesting thing about these last two difficult employee types is that it could be you or I at any at any given time.

Dummy: The dummy category falls into two types;

- Those who don't have the proper training to do the job
- Those that don't have the ability to do the job

For those who need additional training the answer is obvious, get them some training. For those who don't have the ability, the right thing to do is to have a heart-to-heart talk with the person and help him/her find a different position within the company that better fits his/her skills and abilities.

Troubled: Treat this person with tenderness, respect, support and assistance. Virtually everyone has times in their life when they are overtaken by deep personal issues such as

- Severe illness or death of a loved one
- Divorce
- Financial difficulties
- Personal health issues
- Other similar major events.

These events can seemingly overnight make your best employees un-productive, detached or a little self-destructive. As their manager, you are in a position to provide them support, guidance, direct them toward special company resources and generally make their life a little easier (for a short time) until they are able to deal with the personal issues at hand. It's not only the right thing to do as their employer; it's also the right thing to do as a human being.

I had a great long term employee working for me a number of years ago. Her mother was happily living in elderly housing and then had a stroke. To make things worse, her mother's housing facility did not have the capability to provide the care that her mother now needed. My employee, we'll call her Sue, while personally having great difficulty dealing with her mother's failing health, had to quickly find a new living arrangement for her mother. At work, her work quality and volume dramatically decreased.

Seeing and understanding her personal difficulty, I reduced her workload and provided her with a more flexible schedule, thus allowing her to both care for her mother and find her new living arrangements. This went on for about four weeks, at the end of which Sue again became a high producing employee. Also, loyalty to the company was enhanced and the time she missed from work during her difficulty was made up three fold. By acting in this manner, not only did I help the company retain a great employee, but I did the right thing as a human being.

The primary advice and takeaways from today's column is to know that:

- It's possible that there will be a time when you or I may fall into the dummy or troubled category
- If an employee is performing poorly because they are under-trained, provide training
- If an employee is performing poorly because they don't have the ability to do the job, work with them to find something more suitable
- If an employee is in a short-term personally troubled state, if appropriate, try to provide support

Until next time, manage well, manage smart, and continue to grow.

For additional information on today's topic, I suggest the book *Perfect Solutions for Difficult Employee Situations* by Sid Kemp.

COMMUNICATING WITH OTHERS

This may seem like I'm stating the obvious, but being an effective manager requires being an effective communicator. There, I said it. The question for you is, do you agree with my statement? And if so, how do you plan to personally implement it?

Communication comes very easily to some people and is very difficult for others. You should try to find an effective communication process that works well for you, based on your personality, strengths, and weaknesses. The goal of this chapter is not to tell you how you must communicate in a specific manner, but rather:

- To emphasize the importance of quality communication
- To illustrate when and to whom communication is required
- To offer insights into what should and should not be communicated

As a manager you must communicate in multiple directions: up to your manger and other more senior executives, across to your peers, and down to your staff. A failure to properly communicate in any of these directions can be extremely career-limiting.

- If you communicate **up** poorly, you may lose your manager's support
- If you communicate **across** poorly, you may not be seen as a team player by your peers
- If you communicate **down** poorly, your staff's productivity and effectiveness may decline

On the positive side, your ability to properly communicate to these three constituencies can pay off dramatically (both in company performance and, true enough, in your prospects for promotions and salary increases).

The questions to ask yourself when reading this chapter are:

- Do you communicate well up, down, and across?
- Are there things that you could do to better navigate company politics?
- Do you communicate good and bad news on a timely basis?
- Do you properly and effectively promote your department's interests?
- Do you properly and effectively promote the visibility and interests of your staff?
- Are you careful about how you say things to your staff, so that they properly understand your communications?
- Are you careful as to what you say (and how you say it) in emails and other recordable mediums?

Please don't underestimate the positive and negative effect that your communication style and habits can have on your career.

Enjoy the chapter and happy reading.

The importance of communication

By communication, I don't mean talking about Monday night's New England Patriots game against the New York Jets, or perpetuating office gossip, I mean accurately and articulately conveying business related material in an effect manner.

By design, a manager's job is to manage people. This requires telling your staff what to work on and then providing them feedback on their job performance. It also requires that you provide upper management with the status of projects, accomplishments and issues. At a department level, it's also your role to facilitate the coordination with other department such as HR, finance and your peer departments. The bottom line is that the better you communicate, the easier it will be for you to become an effective manager.

Depending on your professional area and your personal strengths and weaknesses, good communication can be a difficult thing to achieve. From an educational perspective, I went to college for accounting and computer information systems. Of the fifty classes I took over four years as an undergraduate student, only one optional elective dealt with personal communication. This was a class on public speaking.

For many of us, particularly those of us in technical roles, we were told that we did such a good job as an individual contributor in our profession area, that we should take a new job (as manager) where we had no formal training, no on-the-job experience, and no formal education on proper business communication. Thus, a new manager was born.

As a manager, communication takes many forms, as outlined below.

- Justify your budget requirements
- Write status reports
- Make presentation to justifying hiring needs

- Giving work direction to your team
- Write and give performance reviews
- Facilitate staff meeting
- Participating in cross-department activities

When looking at the list above, you will see that this manager-based communication comes in three primary forms: written text, formal presentations, and personal interaction. Take comfort in knowing that most people are not great in all three.

The trick for you, as a manager is twofold. First, lead with your strengths. Second, work to improve your weaknesses to an acceptable level by practice, instruction, and ongoing mentoring/support.

I'll use myself as an example, I think I write well (I hope you think so too), but I proofread very poorly. I'm somewhat dyslexic and words like "from" and "form" or missing pronouns in sentences are totally missed by my proofreading eye. Also, I skim received emails, rather than read them deeply.

I compensate for these personal challenges by, if appropriate;

- Returning what could be lengthy written emails with phone calls
- Have my presentations and written documents (including the column) proofread by someone else
- Tell my staff to include the word "important" in the subject line if they want to make sure I read it

The moral of the story here is not to learn what I do, but to understand none of us are perfect. We all have communication-based strengths and weaknesses. Some people hate to do public speaking. Some people consider themselves to be very poor writers. Other people are less comfortable with one-on-one personal interaction.

The trick is that if you just feel uncomfortable communicating, regardless of the communication medium, step outside your comfort zone and try it. You may find that over time your skills improve or you develop procedures to compensate for areas of personal challenge. Who knows, in some cases you may grow to like a previously dreaded activity and move a personal weakness to a professional strength.

The primary advice and takeaways from today's column is to know that:

- There are three primary forms of manager-based communication: written text, formal presentations, and personal interaction
- We almost all have communication-based strengths and weaknesses
- Find ways to use your strengths, and to improve and/or compensate for your communication weaknesses

For additional information on today's topic, I suggest the following book _The Art and Science of Communication: Tools for Effective Communication in the Workplace_ by P. S. Perkins.

Until next time, manage well, manage smart, and continue to grow.

MANAGERS LIVE IN FISH TANKS

Fish tanks? Does this sound strange or what? This is a phenomenon that we have all seen, and the higher level the manager, the worse it gets. People watch, listen and try to figure out the intentions of the managers above them. For example, a senior manager sees you leaving the office at 6:00 PM one night and says to you "Good to see you have been working so hard". Then, you try to figure out what she meant. Did she mean:

- Was she glad you were working late?
- Did she previously think you weren't working hard and you've improved?
- Did your name come up in conversation as a hard worker?
- Did she mean you're up for promotion?
- Was it a subtle warning that you should continue to improve, or else?
- Was she making idle chatter and it didn't mean a thing?

As another example, your manager seems to be spending a lot of time these days with his door shut. Is he looking for a new job? Is he working on something secret? Is he taking daily naps?

The reason why this fish bowl phenomenon exists is because of the power that a manager has over those in his/her group. To a large extent, as a manager, you are making decisions regarding your team's salary raises, promotions, projects, training, and longevity in time of layoffs or company reorganizations. Not to mention, as the manager, you are in a position to foster a safe, energetic environment or make your team members miserable.

Because of this phenomenon, I suggest you watch your words and actions carefully and consider the following:

- Never joke about firing someone, they may not be 100% sure that you are kidding

- Be careful not to use sexual innuendo, otherwise you may find yourself being accused of sexual harassment
- Try not to use a sarcastic tone when complementing your staff members; they may consider it an insult rather than a complement. At minimum, you may leave them confused.
- Be careful when comparing one employee to another employee in their presence. It may be thought of as favoritism and/or may leave both employees feeling uncomfortable and resentful.
- Your staff may also be trying to analyze your emails, general mood, how fast you are walking down the hallway, and anything else that seems interesting.

The above list gives you some tips on what to (and what not to say), but also remember that the words you say are only part of your overall message. Your body language, voice tone, and timing of your message can also play a major role in how your words are interpreted.

As a manager, you are also an employee. That said, how do you look at and listen to your manager? Logic should dictate that the people in your group are looking at you the same way.

The primary advice and takeaway for today's column is to know that:

- Understand that those who report to you are very likely analyzing and reanalyzing your words and action to ascertain their true meaning
- When speaking with your staff members, be very careful of what you say and how you say it. It will help reduce your staff's need to analyze you, reduce their confusion as to your intentions, and generally reduce their stress levels.

For additional information on today's topic, I suggest the following book _Communication Skills for Leaders: Delivering a Clear and Consistent Message_ by Bert Decker.

Until next time, manage well, manage smart, and continue to grow.

BEING THE CHIEF CHEERLEADER
FOR YOUR DEPARTMENT

As the department manager, you should be the number one advocate for your group. It's your responsibility to make sure that your department gets:

- The resources it needs to function properly
- The appropriate respect from other parts of the company
- Recognition for deserving people in your department for a job well done

Regarding promoting yourself, if your team is perceived as efficient, organized, important to the company, as the department manager, it will benefit you personally.

Now here comes the cheerleader part. One way the company will know how well your department is doing is by you telling anyone that will listen. I don't mean being obnoxious about it, just say it in small, appropriate doses. For example, when asked casual questions by senior people in the company, like "How is it going?" don't say "Great, how about you?" Instead, say "Things are going really well, for the fifth month in a row my department is 20% above our quota". Have four or five of these informational nuggets at the ready. These quick informational exchanges can give your department a big boost at unexpected times. For example, the senior executive that you told about your quota in the last example may need a regional manger somewhere, or at the next corporate meeting, that executive may use your department as the example of teams that exceeded their quota.

You should also be the chief cheerleader for the individuals in your group. This builds loyalty within your team toward you and it gives the individuals in your group the recognition they deserve. For example, when your boss asks "How is it going?" you can say "Great, in fact Joe just negotiated a great service agreement with one of our vendors." This type of answer to your boss, or other executive, tells him/her three things:

- First, and the most obvious, is that Joe is going a great job
- Second, is that you are the kind of manager that is willing to give deserved credit to the individual members of your team
- Third, good things are happening within your department and you are smart enough to recognize it

As chief cheerleader, you should also be showing interest, excitement and enthusiasm in your department's role within the company, the work your group is doing and how your group is performing. This enthusiasm will raise the energy level of the people around you, including your team, your peers, and, to a certain extent, your boss.

There is one last place that you should be chief cheerleader, that's for yourself. It is good to be selfless and pass credit on to your group members; it is also very advantageous to be your own chief cheerleader in a humble kind of way. You don't want to say how great you are, because people will just roll their eyes at you. Instead, learn to talk about your successes and accomplishments in a factual and matter of fact way. You can get your point across without appearing to be boasting.

The primary advice and takeaway for today's column is to know that:

- As department manager, it's your job to be the primary advocate for your department in regard to recognition, company respect, needed resources
- As department manager, it's your job to assure that people within your group get appropriate company recognition for their work
- Self promotion is achieved by the combination of promoting your department's and staff's achievements and speaking factually (non-boasting) about your personal accomplishments.

For additional information on today's topic, please refer to my book _Manager Mechanics: Tips and Advice for First-Time Managers_ by Eric P. Bloom.

Until next time, manage well, manage smart, and continue to grow.

MANAGING UP

Managing up is one of the most important things that you must learn to do. To a large extent, the levels of management above you control your success and future at the company. If they like you, respect you, and think that you can help their careers, they will increase your responsibility, promote you, raise your pay and generally make your work life more pleasant. Keep in mind, managing up effectively does not mean kissing someone's backside, sucking up, brown nosing or what ever other cliché you would like to use. Effectively managing up is about the following:

- Communicating news, status, issues, successes, and needs to your manager
- Gaining the trust of your manager in regard to decision making, team leadership, task competency, and other related items
- When appropriate, standing your ground for an important cause, issue, team member need, or customer need
- Producing quality work
- Being responsive to all levels of management as requested or as business necessity requires
- Meeting your deadlines

It also means that if your boss needs a report by Friday, get it to him/her on Friday, or Thursday if you can. If you need additional resources, do your homework and clearly explain why you need them, how much it will cost, and its return on investment (i.e. better analysis, faster service, cost savings, etc.)

Managing up is also the art of using your boss to help you get things done. Generally speaking, if you have good ideas that your boss likes, he/she will help you, if it is within his/her means to do so. After all, when you and your department do good things, it not only looks good for you, it looks good for your boss as well.

The next scenario where managing up is important, is when there are problems. The general rules are:

- Whenever you tell your boss about a problem, also suggest one or more potential solutions
- It is also acceptable to ask your boss for advice on how to handle a particular situation. After all, he/she has more experience than you
- A good manager is also a good teacher and mentor, so seek his/her advice and learn

A strong relationship with your boss will not only help you get the resources and the recognition you may desire, it may also have a profound effect on the relationship and influence that you have with your peer managers. If you have a good relationship with your boss, particularly if it is better than the relationship your boss has with your peers, it puts you in a very powerful position when dealing with your fellow managers.

Lastly, take great comfort in knowing that your boss is on your side. If he is the one that promoted you or hired you into the position, he will want you to succeed. After all, it was his decision that gave you your new job in the first place. As a result, your performance (good or bad) reflects on his/her decision-making ability.

The primary advice and takeaways from today's column is to know that:

- Develop an open, honest, supportive, and communicative relationship with your manager
- A strong working relationship with your boss can help further your career
- If your boss is the one who hired you or promoted you, he/she will want you to be successful because it reflects on his/her decision making ability

For additional information on today's topic, I suggest the following book _Managing Up: How to Forge an Effective Relationship With Those Above You_ by Rosanne Badowski.

Until next time, manage well, manage smart, and continue to grow.

The rule of "no surprises"

In business, if it's not my birthday, surprises are usually a bad thing. Also, a coworker of mine use to say that bad news doesn't get better with time. These two thoughts ring very true in the business arena. When there is an issue within your department, the worst thing you can do is not tell your boss. This may sound counter-intuitive, but it is the best possible course of action for the following reasons:

- When you tell your manager about a problem and propose a solution it lets him/her know that you realize a problem exists and you are thinking of ways to solve it
- All departments have problems. That's why departments need managers.
- If your manager notices a problem within your department that he/she thinks you are not addressing, it may reduce your manager's confidence in your management ability
- When you tell your manager that something is going well he/she will believe you because he/she knows that you also tell him/her when issues arise.
- Your manager has the right to know, it's his/her group also, just at a higher management level
- If your manager finds out about an issue in your department from others, it puts you in a bad situation. You look like you either don't know about it, or that you did know, but didn't want to tell your manager
- Once the problem is fixed, you can take credit for it and add it to the accomplishments section of your annual performance report

Now back to discussing no surprises. As a general rule, good companies can solve or at least mitigate most business problems if they have enough time to react. By raising the issue early, you can help keep the problem small. Also, it lets your boss know that you are paying attention and being proactive, rather than reactive.

Note that this rule of no surprises is true at all professional levels.

- Just as your manager would not like bad news surprises from you, your manager does not like giving bad news surprises to his/her manager.
- When your boss asks "How are things going?" he/she is very possibly looking for a quick fact-based assessment, both good and bad, to say when speaking with his/her manager.

To illustrate this concept, let's say there was in issue with one of the projects in your department, you explain this issue to your boss in your weekly status update meeting, and you also present an appropriate solution to correct the problem. This simultaneously

- Shows your boss that you recognize there is a problem
- Demonstrates that you know how to correct the problem
- Shows that you are willing to tell your boss the good and the bad, which helps build trust
- Provides your boss with the opportunity to help correct the issue
- Gives your boss talking points with his/her boss as to the status of your projects and with luck, discuss his/her confidence in you to recognize and correct business issues

The primary advice and takeaway for today's column is to know that:

- Be honest and straight forward with your manager regarding issues that arise within your department
- Whenever you tell your manager about an issue, also provide one or two possible solutions
- Good companies can generally solve or at least mitigate most business problems if they have enough time to react, so raise issues promptly when they are still small

For additional information on today's topic, I suggest the book *Managing Up: How to Forge an Effective Relationship With Those Above You* by Rosanne Badowski and Roger Gittines.

Until next time, manage well, manage smart, and continue to grow.

MANAGER LEVEL POLITICS

Management level politics are very different from individual contributor politics. As an individual contributor, you can generally stay clear of office politics altogether if you wish. You can just keep you head down and do your work. Politics at the individual contributor level tend to be mostly related to:

- Who gets the best office (or cube)
- Who learns the newest technology
- Who gets the best projects
- Who doesn't get their sales region cut

Simply said, individual contributor politics are about you and your stuff.

Moving from being an individual contributor to a manager is like moving from being single to being married. Now it's not all about you. It's still a little about you, but mostly, it is now about us, you and your spouse, you and your team. As a manager, your ability to play the game not only affects you, but it also affects the people in your department.

As a manager, your politics are still primarily with your peers, but now your peers are the other managers. You will find that your manager peer group is much better at office politics than the individual contributors you used to compete with. You will also find that you will still be fighting for some of the same things, like office space, projects, sales territory and the like, but they will be at the department level, rather than on an individual basis. There will also now, however, be new manager-level politics in areas such as:

- Who works on which company-wide initiatives
- How next year's budget dollars are divided across departments
- Which department gets to hire additional people

- Who's team member gets recognition for outstanding work at the annual company picnic
- Who gets to be the new manager if two groups are merged into a single department

You may also find that some politics go away. For example, within the business analysis group, politics at the individual contributor level revolve around who gets what project. As the manager of that department, by default, you get all the projects. The politicking regarding specific project-related work is now under you. It's your staff who will be fighting to get the best projects.

Most people think of office politics as always being bad, and something to be avoided. Well, sometimes office politics are bad, or at a minimum, expend unneeded energy that could be better spent on company initiatives. Sometimes, however, manager-level politics are actually good for you and/or your department and you should seek to participate. Like it or not, manager-level politics can help you get:

- The resources your team needs to maximize productivity
- Exciting new projects, recognition, promotions, salary raises, and/or bonuses for members of your team
- Permission to hire additional staff so your current team members won't be overworked
- Personal recognition, promotion, salary raises, and/or bonuses

Lastly, office politics with your peers is like sports. You can't win them all. Sometimes you win and sometimes you lose. In either case, learn from what you did right and wrong and also learn from what your peers did right and wrong. Office politics is a place where you really can learn from (and take advantage of) the mistakes of others.

The primary advice and takeaway for today's column is to know that:

- As manager, your ability to play the game not only affects you, but also your department

- Sometimes manager-level politics is good for you and you should seek to participate
- Office politics is like sports, you can't win them all

For additional information on today's topic, I suggest the book _Survival of the Savvy: High-Integrity Political Tactics for Career and Company Success_ by Rick Brandon.

Until next time, manage well, manage smart, and continue to grow.

Knowing what not to send in a business email

Here is the rule. Don't put anything in an email that you wouldn't want your boss, wife, husband, kids, staff, mother, peers, customers and the rest of world to read. Once you press the "Send" key the email is out of your control. Your emails can easily be forwarded to other people inside or outside the company without your knowledge.

That said, I strongly suggest that you do NOT do any of the following:

- **Don't write emails using capital letters**: This is a common email convention that illustrates you are yelling at them
- **Don't write emails that are sexually suggestive**: It's not polite and it could be used as evidence in a sexual harassment lawsuit against you
- **Don't write emails containing mean or bad things about your clients/customers**: They provide the revenue that helps keep you employed
- **Don't write personal related emails from your work computer**: Emails sent, even via your personal email, using company computer resources, gives the company the right to review the content
- **Don't write personal related emails from your work email account**: Depending on your industry, your company emails, even if you delete them, may be stored for audit purposes for up to seven years
- **Don't write or forward racial, sexual, political, or other inappropriate non-business oriented emails from work**: First, business email should be used for business only. Second, you never know who in your office will be insulted, enraged, or disgusted by your email; this can be very career limiting or get you fired. Third, it's very unprofessional and

shows poorly on your character, judgment, and decision making ability.

You really shouldn't do this at all, but if you truly can't help yourself, and find the compelling need to tell someone something mean, bad, unprofessional or just plain obnoxious, either do it in person or over the phone on an unrecorded line. You really don't want that permanently documented and/or passed around the office like a bad joke. It could cost you your job, your personal reputation, and based on the subject matter, it could also be a basis for legal action against you.

As an important note, the same rule also applies to voice mail, online chat, instant messages, text messages and other similar technologies.

All of these rules, do's, and don'ts may seem obvious or a little bit over the top, but they do happen. As an example, I know a manager who received an email that copied many other people, wrote a very inflammatory reply regarding other people on the copy list, and accidently hit "Reply All" instead of "Reply". This was a year-or-two ago and there are still people who have not forgiven him for this email.

In closing, as a manager, you're a representative of the company to your clients and customers. To your staff, you are the voice of authority and their conduit to upper management. As a result, as a manager, your actions, deeds, and missteps regarding email and business activities have greater impact in both positive and negative ways. That said, have you ever written an email that you would be horrified to see on the front page of the Wall Street Journal? It happens.

The primary advice and takeaways from today's column is to know that:

- Be respectful and business-like in your emails. Not only is it the right thing to do, not doing so can cause hard feelings and real damage to you and others
- Business computers and work email accounts should be used for work-related correspondence only

For additional information on today's topic, I suggest the following book _135 Tips on Email and Instant Messages: Plus Blogs, Chatrooms, and Texting_ by Sheryl Lindsell-Roberts.

Until next time, manage well, manage smart, and continue to grow.

THE HIRING PROCESS

As a manager, hiring employees can be your greatest achievement or your biggest mistake.

The reason for making such a strong statement is because, well, it's true. When you hire good people it has the following advantages:

- Shows your manager that you have the ability to hire good people
- Shows your manager that you have good judgment
- Increases your department's overall productivity
- Makes your life easier by not having the issues related to a difficult employee (see Difficult Employees chapter)
- Helps you meet your department's annual goals
- In the longer term, increases your professional network of quality people

The issues related to hiring the wrong people include:

- Making your life much harder by having to deal with the issues related to a difficult employee (see Difficult Employees chapter)
- Making it harder for you to meet your department's annual goals
- Reducing your manager's faith in your judgment
- Adding the inconvenient issues and paperwork related to disciplining and/or terminating an employee

Clearly, spending significant time and effort on the hiring process tends to yield a high return on your investment.

The columns in this chapter discuss various aspects of the hiring process, including getting permission to hire (which is often the hardest part of the hiring process), reviewing resumes, interviewing candidates, and deciding who to hire. It also includes a column that provides various insights into converting contractors into permanent employees.

When reading this chapter, consider the following questions:

- What are the attributes and traits of your most successful hires?
- What are the attributes and traits of your least successful hires?
- What can you do now to help assure you will be given permission to hire future employees when needed (hint: think budgeting and performance metrics)?
- Are there things you can do to improve the way you read incoming resumes?
- Do you have a formalized process to decide which person to hire, or is it strictly a gut feeling?
- Do the job descriptions you use to advertise open positions accurately reflect the actual job responsibilities?
- Is it feasible to hire people first as a contractor before bringing them on permanently? If so, is it worth trying?

Generally speaking, I personally have a pretty good track record for hiring good people. That said, when I look back at my hires that did not go well, I attribute them to two factors: because I didn't pay enough time and attention on the hiring process, and because I settled for a candidate that was good but not great. These are mistakes I hope never to make again. These are easy hiring traps to fall into. Don't let it happen to you and you can greatly enhance your good hire/bad hire winning percentage.

Enjoy the chapter and happy reading.

GETTING PERMISSION TO HIRE

Let's begin with a short lesson on general terminology. In office lingo a job opening is very often called an "open requisition", abbreviated to "open req". If the req is in the budget but not yet open, it is a "budgeted req." If the req is open and you lose the authority to hire, due to a hiring freeze or other issue, the req is referred to as becoming "closed."

Now let's get to the topic at hand. Getting permission to hire is often the hardest part of the hiring process, particularly in today's economy. Gaining this permission is so difficult because most of the factors used to make the decision are outside your control as a manager. These factors include:

- The company's strategic direction
- The company's current profitability
- The company's forecast of future sales and market share
- Your department's function within the company (overhead or revenue-generating)
- If your boss likes you and/or owes you a favor

All that said, being properly prepared and organized when asking to bring a new person onboard can dramatically help your case and should include the following items:

- Writing a quality job description
- Defining the specific business reasons why a new person should be hired
- Calculate the total cost of this new person to the organization (salary, benefits, office space, phone, etc.)
- Theorize the business impact of not hiring this new person (lost sales, missed deadlines, etc.)
- Creation of a formal presentation for your manager containing the above items

The job description is key and should contain the following specific items; the job's title, salary, job duties, eligibility requirements and other similar information. Your Human Resources department should be able to provide you with a few examples. If not, another great source of example job descriptions is to do an internet search or look for a similar type job on your favorite job board such as Monster or Career Builders.

This job description has a number of uses (which is good considering it's a pain to write). These uses include:

- It makes you think about the kind of person you want to hire
- It makes you define the specific duties that need to be performed
- Your boss and/or Human Resources will most likely require it before you are allowed to open the req
- Once permission to hire is granted, Human Resources will use the information contained in the job description to advertise the job and screen incoming applicants.

Now, here are the rules and tricks of the trade when it comes to reqs.

1. As soon as a req opens, work day and night to fill it before it closes.
2. Never hire someone just to get the req filled, you'll soon regret it, wait for the right person
3. Reqs that are in the budget are easier to open than reqs that are not in the budget, so pay attention during budgeting season
4. Reqs that replace a person who left (replacement reqs) are the easiest to get approved
5. A company, no matter how large or successful, can only hire a certain number of people. Very often, success in getting your req open is based on the combination of need and your ability to play company politics

The primary advice and takeaways from today's column is to know that:

- Be properly prepared when asking your manager for an additional hire
- The job description is key and has many uses
- Once your req is opened, move quickly to fill the position
- Never hire the wrong person just to fill the open job, you'll eventually regret it

For additional information on today's topic, I suggest the following book _Smart Hiring_ by Robert W. Wendover.

Until next time, manage well, manage smart, and continue to grow.

Reviewing Resumes

Wow, you got permission to hire an additional person in your group and have some resumes in hand to review. Ok, now what? What is the best way to review a resume?

Everyone has their own way of reviewing resumes. As you gain experience, you will also develop a personal method. Until you develop your own resume screening method, here is a process you can follow. When reviewing this process, understand that your goal is to try to get a mental image of the person.

1. If the resume contains a professional description at the top, read this first. It will give you a quick high level view of the person and potentially provide insight into job fit.

2. Next, by reviewing their education. If they went to a high quality college you know that they are most likely naturally bright. If they didn't attend a top school, it doesn't tell you anything. Some of the smartest most successful people I know did not go to the top schools. It may simply mean that their parents could not afford it.

3. Look for professional certifications. Generally speaking, there are two types of certifications; those that are required by law (or regulation) to perform specified tasks and those that show proficiency in a specified area. These certifications do not necessarily guarantee proficiency, but they do show initiative. Even if they have certifications, if the position requires specific skills, test them on it.

4. Next, look to see if they are active in any professional associations or are a published author (book or professional publication). Activities in these areas show people

are professionally oriented and most likely knowledgeable of the latest industry trends.

5. Next, review their professional experience from oldest to newest. This will give you an idea of the progression of their career.

6. Lastly take a second look at the professional experience and note the following:

   a. See how long the person spent at each company. Unless he/she was a consultant, if he/she hasn't stayed at any one company for more than a year, he/she will probably not stay with you long term.

   b. If in recent years the person has been in multiple jobs and at multiple professional levels, this is very possibly economy related rather than personally related. Lots of companies have closed plants, closed divisions, and/or went out of business. That said, this has caused many, many great people to lose their jobs.

   c. Look to see if they have any interesting items in their background that could be of value. For example, if you are trying to hire an accountant, you may find one that previously worked within your industry.

I have a last suggestion, if you are inexperienced at reviewing resumes, review them with your manager or mentor and ask them their thoughts on each person. You will be surprised how much you can learn about someone when you know how to read his or her resume properly.

The primary advice and takeaways from today's column is to know that:

• When reading a resume, try to get a mental picture of the person being reviewed

- Don't discount people who did not graduate from top schools
- Multiple jobs in recent years is very possibly economy related rather than personal performance related
- If you are unsure about a specific resume get a second opinion

Until next time, manage well, manage smart, and continue to grow.

For additional information on today's topic, I suggest the book *Hire With Your Head: Using Performance-Based Hiring to Build Great Teams* by Lou Adler.

Interviewing Job Candidates

If you think it is nerve racking when interviewing for a job, just wait until you are the interviewer instead of the interviewee. Until you get the hang of interviewing people, you may be as nervous as they are. The trick to giving a great interview and making it a little less scary is to do your homework prior to the interview.

1. Have a strong understanding of the job description. This will allow you to

- Ask questions specific to the job, rather than general in nature
- Better compare the applicant's skills/experience to the job requirements

2. Review the applicant's resume prior to the actual interview. This is important because it

- Shows the applicant that you respect his/her time and that the job is important
- Allows you more time to formulate quality questions based on his/her experience
- Saves you from having to spend time reading the resume during the interview

3. Have an interview plan that includes the following items

- An opening question to put the candidate at ease and begin the dialog on a positive note
- Dialog allowing the candidate to ask questions about the job and/or your company. This will assure that they understand what the job is and you can assess the candidate's interview preparation.
- List of questions related to how his/her experience and skills meet the requirements of the job

- List of questions that will allow you to determine if the candidate's personality is compatible with your department and the company in general
- List of any general questions you always like to ask, like their strengths and weaknesses. You can always use these as a filler if the interview dialog is not going smoothly
- A closing question or statement that allows the candidate to ask any final questions and simultaneously signals that the interview is coming to a close

Many people say that in a thirty minute interview, they decide in the first five minutes (or less) if they like or don't like the candidate. The remaining time is then spent either selling the candidate on the job if they liked him/her, or if they don't like the person, to re-evaluate him/her to make sure their initial instinct was correct.

Some people also like to ask funny questions. I strongly suggest not taking this approach. You may accidently offend the candidate by your question, or just look unprofessional by asking it. For example, I was once asked in an interview "If you could be any type of animal what would it be?" I told him I would be an eagle because it's on the top of the food chain and I could fly for free. He said he liked my answer but that technically an eagle was a bird, not an animal. In any event, he offered me the job.

In closing, it is important that you become a good interviewer. One hallmark of a great manager is the ability to attract and hire great people. Your ability to select the best candidate from a group of applicants and have that person accept the job is directly related to your ability as an interviewer.

The primary advice and takeaways from today's column is to know that:

- Preparation is key to giving a great interview
- Understanding of the job description
- Review the applicant's resume prior to the actual interview

- Have an interview plan
- Your ability to hire the best candidate is directly related to your ability as an interviewer.

For additional information on today's topic, I suggest the book _The Evaluation Interview: How to Probe Deeply, Get Candid Answers, and Predict the Performance of Job Candidates_ by Richard Fear and Robert Chiron.

Until next time, manage well, manage smart, and continue to grow.

Deciding which person to hire

In last week's column I provided some thoughts on the best way to read a resume from a hiring manager's perspective. Well, now that you have reviewed those resumes, orchestrated first interviews for five people and brought two people back for second interviews, how do you decide who to pick? Remember, as a manager one of the most important things you can do for your company, and yourself, is to hire good people.

Below are some suggestions of things you should do and should not do when making your decision.

Things you should consider doing are

- Get advice and input from the other people who interviewed the candidates. Even after years of interviewing and hiring people, I still find other people's points of view about a candidate very valuable.
- Call the candidates references yourself. Managers tend to be more honest and frank with other managers than they are with Human Resource (HR) people. Also, HR people are not subject matter experts in your business area; therefore, you can ask the reference questions that HR can't.
- Consciously consider if the candidate's personality and temperament fit in well with your management style, the team he/she will be working with, and the company's general atmosphere.
- If the candidate is being hired into a technical position, do your best to assure they know the material and can do the job. If you don't personally have the technical skill to assess their ability, have them interview with someone who can.

Things you shouldn't do.

- Don't go against your gut feel. Every time I've done that I've been sorry.

- If neither of your lead candidates meet your need, don't hire one just because he or she is the better of the two possible evils. Start the process over and get more resumes to review.
- Don't make your decision solely based on which candidate is less expensive from a salary perspective. If the best candidate is within your salary range, get the better person.

As additional food for thought, it's been my experience that my best hires over the years have always been smart people, quick studies, and have a great attitude. I've learned not to necessarily pick the person with the best experience and/or credentials. If you hire a person with great credentials and a bad attitude, in six months they'll still have a bad attitude. If you hire a smart person with less experience and a great attitude, in six months not only will they still have a great attitude, but they will also have the needed experience.

As an example, a few years ago I hired a computer programmer that by most accounts was under qualified for the position I had open. I was originally looking for someone with about five years of programming experience. The person I hired only had a year or so of experience, but had an undergraduate degree in applied mathematics from a great school, was naturally very bright and loved to learn. Within a few months he was fully qualified and performing above expectation.

The primary advice and takeaways from today's column is to know that:

- Get advice and input from the other people who interviewed the candidates.
- If none of your current candidates meet your needs, don't just hire one to fill the job, start over and find the right candidate.
- Don't go against your gut feeling. If you don't think a person is right for the job, you're probably right.
- Hire based on personal fit, not just professional credentials.

Until next time, manage well, manage smart, and continue to grow.

For additional information on today's topic, I suggest the book _Finding Keepers: The Monster Guide to Hiring and Holding the World's Best Employees_ by Steve Pogorzelski.

CONTRACTOR TO EMPLOYEE CONVERSIONS

There are many occasions when it makes sense to bring in a temporary employee on a contractual basis. The reason may be that someone is on maternity leave, you may have a seasonal business, or you may be converting to a new computer system and simply need more hands for a month or two. Then, when their task is complete, you let them go as planned. Sometimes however, you decide that you really like this person and decide to convert them from a contractor, to a permanent employee.

Sounds easy right? You like someone's work, offer him/her a job, he/she says yes, he/she starts working for you as a regular employee and all is well with the world. Right? Well, maybe. Many things can potentially make it very difficult or impossible to convert a person from a contracting/temporary role to a permanent position.

To begin, let's assume that you hired this contractor via a contracting company.

These firms generally fall into one of the following four categories.

- No Way
- For a Price
- For a Shrinking Price
- No Problem

The "No Way" firms set up a contractual agreement with the companies they work with, stating that you cannot hire their contractors. They also have the people they represent sign a "non-compete" contract stating that the employee will not accept a job at the companies where they were placed as a contractor for a specified length of time, typically a year. If this is the case, you're stuck and cannot hire that person unless the contracting company owes you a favor.

The "For a Price" firms let you hire their contractors for a price. Generally, after a certain amount of time, typically three months to a year, you can hire their contractor for a specified finder's fee. The fee is typically based on a percentage of the contracting rate. This option gives you the flexibility to hire their people, but it can be very expensive.

The "For a Shrinking Price" firms let you hire their contractors at any time for a fee. The advantage here is that the fee gets smaller over time and is eventually eliminated, usually after six months or a year. The rational behind this arrangement is that it allows your company the flexibility to hire their people at any time, but allows their firm to be reasonably compensated for their efforts. This arrangement is fair to both companies and I like doing business under this type of contract.

The "No Problem" firms let you hire their contractors as an accommodation to the companies they do business with. They ask you (either with a hand shake or contractually) to keep the person as a contractor for a specified length of time, typically three or six months before you hire them. This approach allows them to make a reasonable amount of revenue on the person before they are hired away.

I typically like to work with the "For a Shrinking Price" and "No Problem" type contracting companies because as a manager, they provide me the most flexibility at the lowest price for my company.

The primary advice and takeaways from today's column is to know that:

- There are four types of contracting firms ranging from impossible to easy in regard to permanently hiring the contractors they provide
- Before working with a contracting firm, read their contract and understand your ability to hire the contractors you like

For additional information on today's topic, I suggest the following book *Stop Hiring Failures!* by Steve Springer.

Until next time, manage well, manage smart, and continue to grow.

MANAGEMENT PROCESSES

As an individual contributor, I thought being a manager looked really easy. All you had to do was tell people what to do, give performance reviews once a year, plan and stick to your budget, decide how much to pay people, and go to lots of meetings. Additionally, I felt that if I became a manager I would lose my technical skills and not really replace those skills with anything new.

While it was true that the technical skills I used as an individual contributor did decline, I totally underestimated what I would learn and the skills I would need to be a successful manager.

As discussed in this book's introduction, when I became a manager I found that I had to grow in three ways. I had to learn:

- Leadership
- Management process
- Business process

This chapter discusses management processes. Namely, it discusses various types of management activities that must be performed to keep your department running smoothly and correctly, including budgeting, giving performance reviews, the salary planning process, working with vendors, and some general thoughts on organizational change.

These activities are learned skills, just like computer programming, accounting, and other technical proficiencies. The difference is that at first glance they seem simple. In reality, they are very difficult to do well.

The management-oriented skills discussed in this chapter are by no means a complete list. Because this book is a compilation of one year's weekly columns, there are a number of additional topics that will be discussed in future columns—and (hopefully) in future books.

When reading this chapter, consider the following questions:

- If you are not an accounting person by background and/or training, do you understand the mechanics of your company's budget process and the items contained within your budget?
- Are the people working within your group fairly paid, and is there pay parity among your team members?
- If applicable to your department, are there expenses that you should be capitalizing, not expensing?
- Do you give enough time, thought, and effort to the performance reports you write?
- Are there things you could do to improve the effectiveness of how you work with vendors?
- Are there things you could do to improve your relationship with your finance group and other groups, such as Human Resources and Information Technology?

Doing a great job on your budget, performance review, salary planning, and other similar processes will not only make your department run smoother, but it will also make your manager's job a little easier. Remember, your department is also part of your manager's larger department. Conversely, not performing these tasks well can be very career-limiting. For example, if you had a person working for you that could not effectively manage a small budget, would you give him/her the additional responsibility of managing a big budget? I think not, and neither will your boss.

Enjoy the chapter and happy reading.

Budget planning process

The first step in the budget process is the people in the finance group taking a big sigh and saying "Wow, I can't believe it's budget time already. Between planning next year's annual budgets and calculating this year's actual year end numbers, there will most likely be many twelve hours days until the end of January." The assumption here is that your company's fiscal year goes from January to December.

The first budgeting step that you, as a department manager, will see in the annual budget planning process is an email (or memo) describing the steps you must follow to complete your budget. This email generally includes:

- General budget guidelines
- Step-by-step instructions on each budget phase
- Description of the software used to collect the budget information (which very often is Microsoft Excel ©)
- Dates by which each step must be completed

Pay very close attention to this email and do exactly what it says. If you mess up your budget, not only will you upset your boss and the finance department, but if your budget is done poorly, you will be paying for it all year long. Remember, your next bonus and/or pay increase will most likely at least be partially based on your ability meet your budget numbers.

Generally speaking, the budget process will have two or more phases. The first phase will be you documenting the size of your staff and how much money you think you will need in the upcoming year.

Phase two will most likely comprise of cutting proposed new hires and money out of your budget because your boss and/or the finance group told you to make your budget smaller.

From a timing perspective, let's assume that the company's fiscal year (their financial year) goes from January 1st to December 31st. This being the case, the annual budget cycle probably begins in October for really big companies and in November or December for medium size and smaller companies. The larger the company, the more complex the budget, the earlier they have to start. The reason that budgets in large companies are more complex is because there are more people, organizations, locations and currencies involved in the process.

With the annual budget process complete and the new year upon you, you will begin getting monthly budget versus actual reports. These reports compare what you actually spent to what you budgeted for that month. These numbers are usually shown on a month-by-month and a year-to-date format.

The process of reviewing your budget versus actual numbers should be done as soon as possible each month. The sooner you review your budget reports, the sooner you can make spending adjustments if needed. In addition to this monthly cycle, there is also a quarterly cycle (every three months), particularly if you work for a publicly held company. This is because publicly held companies report their earnings to Wall Street on a quarterly basis.

In addition to the month-by-month review of your budget, changing business conditions often cause companies to reformulate their budgets one or more times during the year. In good times budgets increase. In bad times, budgets are surely reduced. A deep understanding of your budget's mechanics, department goals, and company direction will be of great value to you during these times of mid-year budget modifications.

Then, come next November, you too will be saying "Wow, I can't believe it's budget planning time already. Were did the year go?" Hopefully you will also say. "Wow, I'm about 10% under budget this year. I bet I'll get a great annual bonus.

The primary advice and takeaways from today's column is to know that:

- Take the budget planning process seriously. If it's done poorly you'll be paying for it all year long
- Carefully review your budget-to-actual reports on a monthly basis. The sooner you know there is problem, the sooner you can take steps to fix it.

For additional information on today's topic, I suggest the book _Budgeting for Managers_ by Sid Kemp.

Until next time, manage well, manage smart, and continue to grow.

Components of your budget

When reviewing your department's budget, you will find that the items within it can be categorized into one of three types based on your control to affect them. These categories are

- No Control
- Some Control
- Full Control

Before I explain these three categories, please note they are not official accounting or finance terms. In fact, the accounting and finance managers reading this column may not be able to decide if my categorizations are brilliant and insightful or rather funny, but they are very true.

"No Control" items are costs/expenses you have virtually no control over. These expenses are typically allocations of overhead costs based on number of employees, technology usage, office space size and/or location, etc. such as

- Business insurance
- Employee benefits
- Occupancy (rent, heat, electricity, etc.).

Since you have no control over what the company pays for rent, you can't really be judged on these costs. However, if these costs go up dramatically you may be required to adjust other items in your budget to stay within your overall budget. Your finance person is your best line of defense against problems with "No Control" items. It's the finance department that calculates the allocations. Therefore, your finance person may be able to find a way to minimize the effect of these items on your total budget or at least make sure that you are not penalized for it at bonus time.

"Some Control" items are costs that you have a limited ability to control. Examples of these expenses include payroll, telephone and vendor agreements. Regarding your payroll expense, you obviously have to pay your people, but you can delay hiring. Delaying a hire by a month or two has a very positive effect on your expenses. It not only reduces your actual expense by the salary amount, but it also reduces the costs of benefits, payroll taxes and headcount-based allocations like those previously mentioned.

Generally speaking, the "Some Control" items will be the biggest piece of your budget. Therefore, small percentage savings in this area can give you the biggest gains.

"Full Control" items include items like training, travel (airplanes, hotels, food, etc.), user conferences, professional dues, lunches for noontime meetings and offsite meetings. Unless your department does a lot of required travel, the "Full Control" items tend to be a small percentage of the overall budget, but are the easiest to cut when times get tight. Think of it from a personal perspective, it makes more sense to reduce your personal expenses by bringing lunch rather than by not paying your rent.

Department budgets are funny; I always thought that the bigger my organization and the bigger the budget, the more flexibility I would have on how to spend it. The truth is, I never found that to be the case. Yes, of course there was more money, but generally speaking, the proportion of no control, some control, and full control was roughly the same. Also, with the wider level of responsibility, came increased complexity regarding prioritizing how the money should be spent.

The primary advice and takeaways from today's column is to know that:

- Items in your department budget can be classified as you having no control, some control, or full control over the expenditures
- Knowing which of your budget line items fall into which of the categories can provide you with insights into the best way to manage your budget

For additional information on today's topic, I suggest the book *Budgeting for Managers* by Sid Kemp and Eric Dunbar.

Until next time, manage well, manage smart, and continue to grow.

EXPENSES VERSUS CAPITALIZATION

I'm not a CPA, but I did play one on TV (I really didn't, but I always wanted to say that). As a manager, however, I found that knowing the difference between expensing a purchased item and capitalizing a purchased item occasionally allowed me to purchase more goods and/or services for my department in a given year.

At a high level and from an accounting perspective, when you buy a product or service for your company, it can be accounted for in one of two ways; as an expense or as a capital expenditure. Conceptually, the difference is related to the useful life of the product you purchased. If your purchase will be used within a one year period, then it must be expensed during the current year. However, if the purchased item has a useful life of many years, for example a new truck or a big computer, then from an accounting perspective you can capitalize the purchased item and then expense it over a specified number of years.

In accounting terms, current period expenses must be deducted from your taxes in the current year. Money spent as a long term investment (like a truck or computer) is capitalized, meaning, rather than being expensed in the current year, it is placed on the balance sheet as an asset and then depreciated.

If you have the background to understand what I'm talking about, that's great. If you don't, as a manager you should learn a little about accounting. If you are not already doing so, in time you will most likely be involved in budgeting, salary planning, revenue forecasts, and/or approving company expenses. Sorry to tell you, but all of these activities are accounting related. Taking an accounting class or reading a good book on accounting would be a good personal investment in your professional future.

It would also be worthwhile to ask your company's finance person if any of your department's expenses can, and should, be capitalized.

If the finance person says yes, carefully follow the capitalization instructions. These instructions must be correctly followed because the company may one day be audited to assure that proper capitalization rules were used.

Your first thought may be "Who cares?" The answer is your company's senior management and finance group may really care. First, if the expense is categorized as a expense, there is the potential for company tax advantages. Second, if the company is publicly held, the capitalization of an expenditure not only increases current net income but also increases the company balance sheet.

Your next question may be "Why do I care?" The answer is twofold. First, as a manager you are part of the company's management team and you should want what's best for the company. Second, capitalized expenses are generally budgeted differently than general expenses. Therefore, you may be able to get more money for your department to spend on big stuff, like new computers for your staff. Remember, more money means your department means you can do more things. Generally speaking, investments that make your department more productive are good for your team, your company, and as the department manager, for you.

The primary advice and takeaways from today's column is to know that:

- Knowing the difference between an expense and a capital expenditure may allow you to get more money for your department
- If you don't understand accounting, as a manager, taking an accounting class would be of professional value to you
- Manager processes such as budgeting, salary planning, revenue forecasting, and other manager functions require a certain level of accounting knowledge.

For additional information on today's topic, I suggest the book *The Accounting Cycle: A Primer for Nonfinancial Managers (50-Minute Series)* by Jay L. Jacquet and William C. Miller Jr.

Until next time, manage well, manage smart, and continue to grow.

Working with the Finance department

Companies are in the business of making money. Guess who counts it? You got it, it's the finance department. They also measure your department's finances and you will be judged on their measurements. The key to working effectively with finance people is to understand their world. After all, your department's financial health is a key component of good management.

Your finance person can help you with a number of tasks, including

- Building your initial annual budget
- Describe what expenses other departments charged to your department
- Calculating your quarterly forecasts
- Helping you analyze your budget vs. actual monthly/quarterly reports

Additionally, they can also generally give you very valuable advice on the best ways to manage your costs. I don't mean by telling you to stay in cheaper hotels (even though they do that too) you can figure that one out on your own. I mean that a good understanding of how your company allocates revenues and expenses can greatly assist you in meeting your budget goals. For example, say that you are buying lunch for ten customers that are coming to your office to discuss future software product changes. You may find that if you classify the lunch as a customer meeting, it is automatically charged to the Marketing Department rather then to your Product Development department. Of course the cost to the company is the same, but it saves your budget dollars for lunch on another day. I don't condone doing anything inappropriate, but understanding how these intricacies work within your company, will not only help you spend your money wisely, but help stop other parts of the company from spending you're your department's money wisely. Let's change roles, if you were the Manager of Marketing, wouldn't you like to know that the

Product Development Group was changing lunches to your department?

As a manager, it is important for you to understand

- How your budget in constructed
- The effect that your budget will have on your ability to travel, train your team, hire staff, purchase goods, hire consultants, etc.
- How to read budget vs. actual reports
- The effect that meeting (or missing) your budget has on your annual performance review, raise, and bonus

The finance department can also play an invaluable role during times of growing or declining budgets. In good times when budgets are increasing, they can help you define, justify, and calculate the funding needed for new projects and new hires. In times of declining budgets, they can help you decide the best ways to cut your budget with the least effect on your department's processes and people.

In summary, don't underestimate the value of a strong relationship with the finance department, particularly if you do not have a financial background. As a manager, very few things can get you in more trouble then out of control spending. It could cost you your raise, your bonus, your promotion, or your job.

The primary advice and takeaways from today's column is to know that:

- Your department's financial health is a key component of good management
- The finance group can help you keep your department's expenses on track
- The finance group can also help assure that your budget is designed in a way that will allow you meet your department's goals.

Until next time, manage well, manage smart, and continue to grow.

Performance reviews

Performance reviews are one of the most important things a manager can do for the people in his department. Take them seriously, complete them on time and be honest, constructive, critical, complimentary and sincere. Just like you have probably read and re-read your annual reviews, so will your subordinates.

Every company seems to have its own version of a performance review form. That said, generally they fall into one of the following three categories.

- Narrative-based
- Quantitative-based
- Narrative/ Quantitative combination

Narrative-based performance reviews usually include a list of the person's prior year accomplishments, their strengths and weaknesses, a personal development/training plan for the coming year and a short summary of the person's overall performance.

Quantitative-based performance reviews are generally either a list of statements that you "Strongly agree", "Agree", "Disagree" or "Strongly disagree" with, or a list of attribute types like "Leadership ability", "Quality of work", "Timeliness" that you rate on a scale from 1 to 10.

Narrative/Quantitative combination performance reviews are what you would expect, a review document containing both narrative and quantitative components.

These review styles all have the same intention, to provide the employee with an accurate and honest assessment of his/her personal performance during the prior year. It should also be forward thinking and contain an action plan to assist the employee in growing professionally, and sometimes even personally.

Lastly, delivery of the review document should not be considered to be the end of the review process. It should be viewed as the basis for a two-way conversation between the manager and his/her subordinate.

- If a person is doing a good job, they deserve to be told
- If a person is doing a bad job, they deserve to be told
- In both cases, as their manager, it's your job to tell them

It's also your job to tell the person where improvements are needed. Then, work with the person to formulate a plan to make those improvements. These plans generally include a combination of formal training classes, on-the-job experiences and things to personally work on, like attitude and level of effort.

I believe in the philosophy that

- No one is so good that you can't find something that needs improvement
- No one is so bad that you can't find something good to say

When I write someone's review, regardless of the format, I make sure to discuss both their good points and their bad points. If you say only good things in a review, you may be helping their ego, but you are not providing them any tangible value. As a result, you are really doing the person a disservice. If you only say bad things, even if they are meant in a constructive way, the person will just feel beat up and not take your criticism to heart.

Writing a good review for your staff is actually very good for your career for a number of reasons

- The people in your group will appreciate your effort and be a little more loyal to you
- You want to be known as a good manager, and good managers write good reviews
- It's always a good idea to impress the people in Human Resources

- Well written constructive criticism can improve employee performance, allowing your department to run more efficiently
- If someone is performing poorly, their review serves as documentation toward their removal
- It will be easier to hire quality internal candidates if your reputation is as a good manager

The primary advice and takeaways from today's column is to know that:

- Your team worked all year, they deserve an hour or two of your time to write an appropriate annual review
- Quality reviews will help you gain the loyalty and respect of your team
- Being known as a good manager, including writing quality reviews, will help you professionally

For additional information on today's topic, I suggest the book _The Essential Performance Review Handbook: A Quick and Handy Resource For Any Manager or HR Professional_ by Sharon Armstrong.

Until next time, manage well, manage smart, and continue to grow.

Giving raises

As Tom Cruise said in the movie Jerry McGuire "You complete me", oh sorry, I meant "Show me the money", Ah, ya, that's the one, "Show me the money". That said, giving raises is not just about the money; it's also about the message behind the money.

For example, is 5% a good raise? The short answer is yes, it would be nice to get a 5% raise. Now let's put it in perspective by the following two statements. "Hi Mary, congratulations on your 5% raise, I want you to know that the average raise this year was 2%. You got 5% because of your outstanding work over the past year."

Compare that statement to this statement. "Hi Mary, we gave you a 5% raise this year. The average raise was 8%. You only received 5% because your work was not of the quality it has been in past years. Let's sit down next week and talk about an action plan that will help you return to your previous top performance."

Changing topics to the salary planning process, pay raises are generally scheduled in one of two ways.

- Raises given on the anniversary of hire date
- Raises given to everyone in the company at the same time

If your company gives people raises on their employment anniversary, then the math is simple. You'll be given a general guideline/formula that considers the person's performance, current salary and other various factors. For the most part, you follow the formula, and it tells you the raise amount. For example, let's consider the following very simple formula:

- Top performers get a 4% raise
- Average performers get a 3% raise
- Below average performers get a 2% raise
- Bad performers get no raise at all

Using this formula, if you consider the employee to be an average performer, he/she gets 3%. This simple formula is for illustration only and of course did not consider the person's current pay rate and other important company specific factors.

In companies that give all employees pay raises at the same time, you generally will also be given a guideline like the previous example. But in this case, you will also generally be given a budget amount based on a percentage of your department's total annual payroll. For example, if your department's total annual payroll is $100,000 and the average raise should be 4%, you will then have a $4,000 pay raise budget to divide among the members of your group.

The use of a budgeted raise amount has two major ramifications.

- First, if everyone in your department is making about the same amount, if you give a 5% raise to one person; then you must give someone else a 3% raise to stay within budget.
- Second, the higher someone's pay is as compared to the average, the greater effect that person has on your overall budgeted dollars. For example, if Joe is making $20,000 and Sally is making $40,000, each 1% pay increase will cost $200 for Joe and $400 for Sally.

Your job as the department manager will be to combine the math, team member performance, department goals and company goals to create a pay raise plan that that is fair to your team members, considers company goals, and meets your budget.

The primary advice and takeaways from today's column is to know that:

- The message about the raise is as important as the raise itself
- In many cases, salary planning is a zero-sum-game; the more you give to one person the less you can give to someone else
- Make sure you understand and follow company guidelines

For additional information on today's topic, I suggest the following book _Performance Appraisals and Phrases For Dummies_ by Ken Lloyd.

Until next time, manage well, manage smart, and continue to grow.

GIVING PROMOTIONS

Giving someone a promotion sounds like it should be easy. You call the person into your office, tell him he has been promoted and to continue doing great work, shake his hand and send him on his way. In one sense, it is that easy. However, there are a number of factors to consider when deciding who to promote and when to promote them. Additionally, there are a number of ramifications associated with giving someone a promotion and they're not all good.

When deciding if someone should be promoted, consider the following:

- The person himself
- The role the person plays within the department
- The effect the promotion will have on the other members of the team
- The department's current situation.

Let's begin with the person himself. The first and most obvious question is this person worthy of a promotion. The answer to this question surrounds the length of time he/she has been in the job, his/her competency, his/her attitude, has his/her skills grown beyond the current job title, and your desire as the manager to promote him/her.

Regarding the person's role within the department; is the person a natural leader within the group, is the person taking on more responsibility, are other people in the group seeking out this person's technical expertise and/or advice.

Regarding the effect the promotion will have on the department, you have to consider how other members of the team react to this person's promotion. Will they agree and be supportive or will they be upset and/or feel the promotion was unwarranted and unfair. Other thoughts, such as "If I promote Joe, should I also promote Mary" are very common and must be considered.

Regarding the department's current situation, if the department just failed on a major project, it's not a good time to promote someone no matter how good they are.

When you promote someone, you are telling that person, and the rest of your team, that the person being promoted embodies the desirable qualities, attitudes and attributes that facilitate recognition and promotion. As a result, you are not-so- subtlety telling the rest of your staff to act in the same manner. Promoting someone is the strongest statement you can make to the other people of your team how to act if they would also like to be promoted.

Remember, promotions are not only a show of support and recognition toward the person who received it; they are also a statement and motivator (or de-motivator) to those who were not promoted.

Lastly, the decisions you make regarding who should and/or should not be promoted will be used by your boss to assess your decision making ability. So, be fair, unbiased, and analytical when making promotion related decisions; if not, you may find yourself being passed over on your next potential promotion.

The primary advice and takeaways from today's column is to know that:

- Promotions should be given in a fair and unbiased way
- Think carefully how other members within the department will view the promotion
- Promoted people that embody the qualities, attitude, and attributes that are valued within your organization

For additional information on today's topic, this week, I suggest my book _Manager Mechanics: Tips and Advice for First-Time Managers_ by Eric P. Bloom.

Until next time, manage well, manage smart, and continue to grow.

SALARY PLANNING

My goal in this week's column is not to make you a salary planning expert. We will leave that to the Human Resources and compensation professionals. The goal here is for you to gain a general understanding of various salary planning fundamentals so you can effectively participate in your department's salary planning process.

The fundamentals of salary planning include **Job Descriptions, Job Levels, Salary Ranges, Salary Surveys, Position in Salary Range,** and **Salary Range Quartiles**.

A **Job Description** is a description of the job, including its title (the name of the job, for example, Business Analyst), responsibilities, tasks, needed skills, required certifications and needed level of experience. The job description is the primary communication vehicle of the job's responsibilities. The job description is also the basis for defining the **Job Level** and **Salary Range**.

A **Job Level** is where the job fits within the company hierarchy. For example, the Business Analyst job family may go from *Junior Business Analyst* to *Senior Business Analyst* to *Principal Business Analyst*. As a result, the job description for a *Senior Business Analyst* should require more experience than the job description for a *Junior Business Analyst*. Once a job is leveled, it has to be assigned a **Salary Range**.

A **Salary Range** is the range of pay that the company is willing to pay for a specific job. For example

- The range of pay for a *Junior Business Analyst* may be from $40,000 to $60,000
- The range of pay for a *Senior Business Analyst* may be from $50,000 to $80,000

Conceptually, these salary ranges are determined by a number of factors including

- Needed skills
- Required certifications
- Amount of experience
- Level of responsibility

In reality, the salary range associated with a job tends to be driven by

- General market conditions
- Supply and demand for the specified skill set
- What other local companies are paying for similar jobs

As an added point, sometimes specialized skills demand higher salary ranges, For example, knowledge in new computer software technologies tend to bring a higher price than the equivalent skills in standard or older technologies.

Many Human Resources departments define their salary ranges with the help of **Salary Surveys**. These surveys are facilitated by consulting firms that collect, aggregate and analyze salary data from hundreds of companies. Then, they summarize the collected information by job type and sell it back to the participating companies. The companies then use it as a reference guide to define their salary ranges.

Once a job's salary range has been defined, the general rule of thumb regarding where a person should be **Positioned in a Salary Range** is a

- Less experienced person should be in the lower end of the salary range
- Fully qualified person should be in the middle of the range
- Very experienced person should be in the higher end of the range

Some companies break salary ranges into **Salary Ranges Quartiles**. Quartiles are four smaller ranges within the salary range. For example, as discussed earlier, if the "Junior Business Analyst" salary range goes from $40,000 to $60,000, the quartiles would be $40,000 to $45,000, $45,001 to $50,000, $50,001 to $55,000 and $55,001 to $60,000.

With the range quartiles defined, people's pay raises are then partially based on their quartile within the range. The rationale being if are fully qualified

- You should be at midpoint
- If paid less than midpoint, you are underpaid and should receive a larger than average increase
- If paid more than midpoint, you should get a smaller increase because you are already being appropriately compensated

Sorry for all the math and numbers, but welcome to management. If needed, ask your Human Resources person for help. It's their job to help you.

The primary advice and takeaways from today's column is to know that:

- The fundamentals of salary planning include Job Descriptions, Job Levels, Salary Ranges, Salary Surveys, Position in Salary Range, and Salary Range Quartiles.
- You don't need to be an expert in these fundamentals, but as a manager you do need to understand what they are
- If you have trouble with the math, Human Resources can help

Until next time, manage well, manage smart, and continue to grow.

PARITY IN PAY AMONG PEERS

The goal of "parity in pay" is that everyone doing more or less the same job should receive more or less the same pay, with adjustments based on experience and other appropriate factors.

That said, people are often compensated at different levels, even within the same department for doing basically the same work. I don't mean that this is being done in a divisive, prejudicial or conspiratorial way. Very often, people's professional and company history can cause them to be paid very differently. For example, if Mike was hired when the job market was bad and Mary was hired a year later when the job market was good, chances are Mary will be making a little more money than Mike. This is because Mary would not have joined the company at Mike's salary because she had other job offers pending.

As another example, say Joe and Sally were both hired a year ago. Joe was hired as the manager of a different department, and Sally was hired as a Junior Analyst. Joe then did a poor job managing his department and was moved into an individual contributor role as a Senior Analyst. Sally on the other hand did a great job and was promoted to Senior Analyst. Chances are the company didn't reduce Joe's pay when he became an individual contributor. The chances are also good that Sally got an excellent raise because of her promotion and great performance, but is still below Joe's original manager salary.

The bottom line is that Joe and Sally are basically doing the same job, but Joe is being paid a lot more than Sally. As a department manager, these are the kinds of pay problems you will have to address.

- Your first goal is to recognize that parity in pay issues exist
- Your second goal is to work with your boss and/or Human Resources to correct the issue

Very often these types of issues tend to work themselves out over time. As an example, let's again look at Sally and Joe. Over time, Sally will tend to get bigger raises then Joe because she is doing great work and is being paid less than her peers. Joe on the other hand will tend to get less than average increases because he is being highly paid (maybe over paid) for his responsibilities as an individual contributor, rather than as a manager.

When analyzing your department's salaries consider the following questions:

- Are the members of your team fairly compensated for the work being performed?
- Are team members who are doing similar work compensated at a similar level?
- Are the differences in pay warranted based on level of experience, job knowledge, task efficiency, and other appropriate criteria?
- Are there salary adjustments I should make to assure that all members of my team are paid fairly?

The primary advice and takeaways from today's column is to know that:

- People in similar jobs should be given similar compensation
- If inequities exist, work with your manager and Human Resources to correct the issues
- In many cases, differences in pay are based on work history, rather than for divisive reasons; in any case however, the issue should be recognized, addressed and corrected

For additional information on today's topic, I suggest speaking to your manager and Human Resources representative.

Until next time, manage well, manage smart, and continue to grow.

Organizational Change

When people think about organizational change, it seems that the same old sayings always to come to mind.

- The more things change the more they stay the same
- The only constant is change

Even though I don't personally like these sayings, having been employed by corporate America for most of my life, I have found them to generally be true. That said, I believe these sayings to be self defeating, look at organizational change as an ongoing negative, and provide no value when a changing work environment is thrust upon us.

I like these expressions much better.

- Change brings both risk and potential reward
- Those that embrace change can profit by it

I find these expressions to be forward thinking, energizing when faced with change, and helpful when trying to instill a positive attitude in others.

Companies change for many reasons. Some organizational change is self-induced, meaning the company management has made the decision to strategically move in a specified direction. Sometimes however, change is forced upon a company in order to survive.

That said, organizational change may be initiated for various reasons including the following:

- Company mergers and buyouts, and takeovers
- Market pressure caused by innovative competitors
- Changes in the economy, both good and bad
- Change in company leadership
- At a micro level, maybe you just got a new boss

Early in my career, I worked for a large software company and truth be told, I loved working there. Then one day, our parent company bought our major competitor and merged the two firms. As a result, there was an enormous amount of change. As you would expect, there were winners, there were losers, but for most of us work just continued.

When I eventually left that company, I went to work for a large insurance provider and laughed to myself that this company was much too big to be bought out or merged with another firm. Well, I was right, but guess what they did? They outsourced the Information Technology (IT), the department I working in, to a vendor. This change ended up being more tumultuous to me personally than the merger at the software company.

All that said, my suggestion to you is

- Be resilient
- Embrace change
- Know that in time a new standard norm will emerge

Regarding being resilient, my belief is that resiliency plays an enormous role in our journey both professional and personal. There are very few people blessed lives that are never faced with difficult circumstances. For me personally, there is a quotation by Vivian Greene that has always brought me strength.

- "Life is not about waiting for the storms to pass... It's about learning how to dance in the rain."

Regarding embracing change, if a company has made the decision to change direction, either willingly or unwillingly, as a manager, you are a member of the management team. Therefore, for better or worse, it's your job and responsibility to help your company make the transition. On the positive side, I have seen managers who embraced a new company direction and personally profited by it. On the negative side, I have also seen managers who refused to follow the company's new direction and were eventually cast aside.

Lastly, as stated above, in time a new normalcy will take effect, until of course, the next big change is dramatically presented.

The primary advice and takeaways from today's column is to know that:

- When organizational change is thrust upon you be resilient, help facilitate the change
- As a manager, it's your job and responsibility to help your company make the transition
- Very often, those that embrace change can profit by it

For additional information on today's topic, I suggest the book _Strategic Organizational Change_ by Michael Beitler.

Until next time, manage well, manage smart, and continue to grow.

Working with vendors

I cannot over emphasis the importance of learning how to effectively work with vendors. By managing vendor-related projects well, you can help your departments meet its deadlines. Also, by negotiating well, you can save your company a lot of money.

Vendors can be categorized into two types; providers and strategic partners.

- Providers are companies were you buy stuff (stuff of course being the technical term for business related supplies and materials)
- Strategic partners are companies that play an important role in your success or the success of the company.

Examples of "provider" vendors are the office cleaning company, your office supply vendor (pens, paperclips, etc.) and catering company that delivers company lunches. Examples of "strategic partner" vendors include companies that provide the raw materials for your products, offshore customer service centers and software companies that support for your core business processes.

Provider-type vendors are generally judged on

- Price
- Reliability
- Customer service
- What I refer to as the pain-in-the-neck factor.

Reliability is the vendor's ability to deliver the correct products on time at the agreed upon quality.

Customer service is the ability to respond to your needs and to deliver on their promises. As an example of quality service, if they accidentally deliver the wrong printer toner, will they send you the right toner overnight express, at their expense, so your copy machines don't stop working.

Pain-in-the-neck factor refers to how easily it is to deal with the vendor and how often they aggravate you. Examples of aggravating situations include, taking four months to get your bill right, shipping the product to the billing address and sending the bill to the shipping address, having three different sales people call you on the same day and making you fill out needless and/or redundant paperwork.

At the end of the day, the only one of these items that you can really negotiate is price. The vendor's internal workings and management ability usually define the rest.

When negotiating with provider-type vendors, negotiate on price, based on problems that you have had in reliability, quality of customer service and pain-in-the-neck factors. Of course at some point, if the vendor just can't do the job, find a new vendor, even if it cost you a little more money.

Strategic partner-type vendors are judged on different criteria based on the product or service they provide. For example, if your company assembles pens, then it is very important for the ink cartridges to be delivered on time.

Generally speaking, negotiations with strategic partner-type vendors include the creation of a Service Level Agreement (SLA). An SLA describes in detail the level of service that will be provided by the vendor. For example, a call center based SLA may specify that all incoming calls must be answered within three rings. Another SLA example is that specific raw materials must be delivered within a specified time after the order is placed. Very often the commitments specified in the SLA will be a major impact on the price. For example, a four hour guaranteed response from a service vendor will generally cost more than a twenty-four guaranteed response.

As a last thought, when dealing with your strategic partner-type vendors, cost is certainly always a factor. However, the vendor's ability to deliver is much often more important, because if the vendor fails, it will have an adverse affect of your customers and/or your internal company operations.

The primary advice and takeaways from today's column is to know that:

- Develop strong working relationships with your vendors is key to your success
- There are two primary types of vendors; providers and strategic partners
- Provider vendors provide non-mission products and services
- Strategic partner venders provide the critical products and services needed to run your business
- Maximize your vendor relationships by knowing the difference and treating them appropriately

For additional information on today's topic, I suggest the following book *Supplier Evaluation & Performance Excellence* by Sherry R. Gordon.

Until next time, manage well, manage smart, and continue to grow.

PRIVACY, PROMISES, GOSSIP, AND JOKES

The columns in this chapter deal with various things that happen by accident, through a lack of foresight, and/or through a lapse in judgment. But, as understandable and human as such things are, the person on the receiving end of these issues can feel unfairly treated, misled, and/or violated.

Managing people can be a funny thing. It's easy to say things with the best of intentions that end up having disastrous outcomes. For example, you promise an employee that if they do something good you will reward them in a specific way—a raise, a promotion, attendance at a conference, the chance to work on a great new project, etc. When you can't deliver, the employee feels lied to. Alternatively, through a lapse of judgment you gossip about a member of your team or tell a racial joke that a team member considers offensive. To you it may just feel like an uncomfortable and accidental mistake, but the injuries it may create can be difficult or impossible to correct.

Consider this short story:

Two men, Mike and Joe, live and work in the same city. Mike lives on the north side of town and works on the south side of town. Joe lives on the south side of town and works on the north side of town. As a result, Mike and Joe pass each other on the sidewalk every morning and afternoon on their way to and from work.

After a few months, Mike and Joe notice this patterns and wave hello as they pass on their way to and from work. After a few more months, they learn each other's names and actively greet each other. Once, on an extremely cold day, they stop together at a coffee shop to warm up before continuing to their respective jobs.

As time goes on, they begin looking forward to passing each other on the street; when on a journey, regardless of its length, it feels nice to see a friendly and familiar face.

One day, Mike and Joe stop for some coffee on their way home from work. On the TV they overhear a news item about a political candidate, which inspires a conversation between the two men that eventually grows quite heated. Finally, Mike loses his temper. He threatens and insults Joe, and then he leaves in a huff. The next morning, when they pass each other, Mike apologizes profusely. He takes back everything he said, he'd had a terrible day at work and he didn't mean any of it. They resume their friendship, but Joe never looks at Mike the same way again.. Because of that episode, Joe always looks at Mike a little differently and is a little on guard whenever they pass.

The moral of the story is that when someone is wronged by another person, even if it's an accident or a fluke, it can be almost impossible to completely overcome the episode.

Business relationships can be a lot like this. Once a business relationship is strained by the types of things discussed in this chapter, lost trust can be hard to rekindle.

When reading this chapter, consider the following questions:

- Are you unintentionally making promises to your staff or others that you cannot keep?
- Are there things you could do, or should do, to protect your staff from hurtful office gossip?
- Do you properly safeguard confidential employee and/or customer information?
- Do you tell jokes in the workplace that could be considered offensive by those you work with?

- On the positive side, are there things you can do to enhance the trust, tolerance, and well-being of those on your team?

Enjoy the chapter and happy reading.

PROTECTING EMPLOYEE DATA

As an individual contributor, if you handled sensitive data, it was most likely data about your clients. As a manager, you will also be handling data related to the people that report to you. Here is the lesson; Handle employee data very carefully.

As an example, consider the process of giving employees pay raises. It is very common for people performing basically the same job to be paid very differently because of their professional background, length of time with the company, and other business related factors. That said, if it is salary planning season and your team comes into your office for a staff meeting and all of their salaries are sitting face-up on your desk or displayed on your computer screen, major employee issues could quickly arise.

To prevent this type of issue from occurring, when you leave your office, even just to get coffee, get in the habit of turning on your computer screen saver and remove sensitive documents from your desktop. You don't have to be paranoid about it, just smart. As a manager, you will be handling various types of sensitive company and employee documents. These documents include salary planning documents, performance reviews, tuition reimbursement forms, succession planning details, and/or new hire offer letters. It is best to keep them as private as possible.

A number of years ago I had an office designed in such a way that when sitting at my desk, my back was toward the door. Even worse, my computer screen was also facing the door. I was working on a subordinate's annual performance review and another subordinate quietly walked into my office and started reading it over my shoulder. When I finely saw him, he said that he wasn't looking at my computer screen. He said that he just didn't want to interrupt me. It was very obvious that he was not being completely honest, but it was not something I could have definitively proved. From that time forward, I have always tried to position my desk so I could see people entering my office and not face my computer screen toward the office doorway.

As a side thought on this topic, when at the office, also be careful how you handle your personal and professional data. For example, if you are writing your resume, even if it's to apply for another position inside your company, don't leave it on your computer screen, and don't leave a printed copy of it on your desk. This may seem like obvious advice, and it is. But people can develop a sense of ownership over their office and as a result treat it like personal space. At the end of the day, it's still company property and there are business reasons why your staff, your peers, or your boss may be there without you. For example:

- You scheduled a meeting in your office with a staff member and you are running late. So he/she sits in your office waiting for you.
- Your boss has an urgent document that he/she wants you to see as soon as you return to your office so he/she puts it on your chair.

Here are some additional examples on how to help assure you are properly protecting your company's, client's and employee's information.

- Get in the habit of keeping the documents you are working with in file holders and only take them out of the folders when you are actively working on them.
- Print as little material as possible. This not only saves on paper, but if it's not printed, you can't leave it on your desk.
- If you are working on a particular section of a document on your computer and want to see it printed, just print that section not the entire document. Then, when done with the paper, immediately shred it.

- If you copy a document at the copy machine always double check that you didn't leave the original copy on the machine. I've seen this happen, and it was their resume.

The primary advice and takeaways from today's column is to know that:

- Handle employee data very carefully. If not, it can cause very serious issues for you and/or your staff.
- Develop good habits regarding handing sensitive data. If you do it automatically, then you are less likely make a mistake.

Until next time, manage well, manage smart, and continue to grow.

Making promises you can't keep - Part 1

There is an old expression that says, "No good deed will go unpunished." When trying to motivate a subordinate, hire a new employee, promote a staff member, or help out a customer or vendor, you can promise to try, but never promise that you can deliver, unless it is in your personal authority to do so.

- If you promise to give a subordinate a raise and then can't deliver, you may
  - Lose credibility with that individual
  - Lose credibility with your staff, because people talk, particularly if they're not happy
  - Lose a good employee
  - End up in trouble with your boss or Human Resources
- If you promise something to a customer and can't deliver, you may lose a sale, or lose the customer
- If you promise something to a vendor and can't deliver, it may destroy a vendor relationship, and/or cause lawsuits

Should any of the above situations arise, you have most likely caused harm to a fellow employee, your company, a customer, a vendor, or yourself. For you personally, based on the severity of the issue, you may receive a verbal reprimand, receive a written warning, or even potentially lose your job. Remember, as a manager, you are a representative of your company to the external world and the voice of the company to those that you manage.

As an example of a promise gone very wrong, say that you promised to hire someone. On this promise, the job candidate quits their old job and then to your surprise, your company announced a hiring freeze before the final paperwork was approved. This poor person is out of work because of you. He/she may just yell and scream at you, your manger, Human Resources, and anyone else that would listen, or he/she may sue the company. In any case, you have caused major personal problems for the person you were trying to hire and have made yourself look ineffective and incompetent as a manager.

There are some specific circumstances when you can generally promise things to the people in your group. These include:

- When you get written permission ahead of time from Human Resources, your boss, or other appropriate authority
- When it is included in writing as part of an offer letter given to an employee when first hired
- If there is a written company policy stating that an employee receives a raise, promotion, or other reward if certain criteria are met

I once had a manager that promised I would receive a bonus if a project I was leading went well and was delivered on time. The project went well and was delivered on schedule, but I never received my bonus. As a result, I lost respect for a manager and eventually transferred to another department. In retrospect, I don't know if he tried to get me a bonus and was unsuccessful, never bothered to follow up on his promise, or never originally intended to give me a bonus. That said, to me as the employee, it was all the same.

The primary advice and takeaway for today's column is to know that:

- You can promise to try, but never promise that you can deliver, unless it is in your personal authority to do so
- If you fail to deliver a promise you will most likely cause harm to a fellow employee, your company, a customer, a vendor, or yourself

For additional information on today's topic, I suggest the book _Management Ethics (Foundations of Business Ethics)_ by Norman E. Bowie and Patricia H. Werhane.

Until next time, manage well, manage smart, and continue to grow.

Making promises to your staff that you can't keep - Part 2

When you promise something to an employee, they take it as a done deal. For example, if you promise a promotion to a staff member at the completion of a project, he/she will be expecting a promotion at project end. If you can't deliver, then at best, you have lost credibility, at worst; the employee will be on his way to Human Resources or his/her lawyer to complain.

As another example, if you tell a staff member that if he/she works through the weekend then he/she can go to an up-coming user conference, then don't let him/her go. Not only will you lose personal credibility, but you will never get the person to work another weekend.

By making promises you can't keep, I don't mean to imply that you are purposely lying to your staff. I mean that you should carefully consider your ability to keep your side of the bargain. That said, if you continually fail to follow through on your promises, even if it truly is with the best intentions, you will eventually be viewed as either a liar or ineffective.

Early in my career, I made this mistake. As a young and new manager, I told a member of my staff, Mike, that if he worked on a Saturday to finish a specific project, I would give him a day off during the next week to make up for working Saturday. He worked on Saturday and did a great job. That Monday, I had a meeting with my boss and told him the project was done because Mike had come in over the weekend. I then said I told Mike he could have a day off during the week to make up for his weekend efforts. My boss then said giving time off during business hours for time spent during non-business hours was against company policy.

I felt terrible for telling Mike he could have a day off and my boss was upset with me for not checking the company rules before offering this arrangement. My boss then told me to go talk to Mike. Mike, who had been at the company much longer than I, said he knew the policy and thought it was odd that I made the offer and figured the day off would never happen anyway.

The moral of this story is that even though I tried to do the right thing, my lack of knowledge of company policy and inexperience as a manager caused me to make a promise I couldn't keep. I was fortunate that my boss just considered it to be a learning moment for a new manager and Mike was forgiving of my error, but it could have been much worse. Also, as a young manager, I learned an important management lesson. Before making a promise to a staff member, be positive you can follow up on your promise.

Know that this issue doesn't just happen to new managers. I was also on the other side of this issue as the employee and my boss was a VP level executive. There was an organizational change coming and my boss promised me that I would be receiving additional responsibility. When the organizational change materialized, the size of my boss's team was cut in half. As a result, I ended up with less, rather than more responsibility.

My boss had no idea that the organizational change would affect him in this way. He thought he was going to get more responsibility, not less. He felt personally betrayed by his manager over the change and even worse for not being able to follow through on promises he made to me and his other managers. He eventually left the company.

The primary advice and takeaways from today's column is to know that:

- Don't make promises to your staff you can't keep, you will lose credibility and potentially end up in real trouble
- You can promise to try, but don't promise to deliver unless you are 100% sure it is within your authority to do so

For additional information on today's topic, please read my book _Manager Mechanics: Tips and Advice for First-Time Managers_.

Until next time, manage well, manage smart, and continue to grow.

MAKING RACIAL, SEXUAL OR OTHER JOKES
IN BAD TASTE WITH YOUR STAFF

Hey, did you hear the joke about the you-know-who that did the you-know-what?

How about this one, did you hear the one about the guy who told a racial joke in the office and lost his job? How about the one about the guy who told a sexually oriented joke in the office and was sued for sexual harassment?

Off color jokes have a way of unexpectedly offending people. It may be because

- A coworker is a member of the group being picked on
- You are making needless fun of a group or type of person the coworker loves
- There are simply many people that hate jokes that hurt people

My advice to you is to keep dirty jokes, racial jokes and all other inappropriate jokes and comments out of the office. Not only is it in bad taste, but it may also be illegal.

Twice in my career I have seen people get into real trouble telling jokes they thought were funny in front of fellow employees. Both cases ended with similar results.

- Some thought the jokes were funny and were glad he told them
- Some liked the jokes but thought it was inappropriate to tell them in the office
- Some disliked the jokes because they were of bad taste
- Some were silently offended by the joke
- One or two were not silent in their contempt for the jokes and the person who told them

In one case, the joke teller lost his job. In the other case, he received a written warning from Human Resources.

You should also avoid sending dirty jokes from your work email account or via your personal email account from company equipment. In both of these cases, your company has the right, and in some cases the legal requirement, to monitor your emails.

Not only can emails be easily forwarded without your knowledge, but they also permanently document the fact that you sent the joke though the office. For the record, emails can be used as an exhibit in law suits. Lastly, just because you delete an email from your work email account, it doesn't mean that it's actually gone. Many companies save all sent and received emails for up to seven years. This is done for business purposes, usually for regulatory or business reasons, but this business process can also be used to retrieve your emails for disciplinary investigations.

I spent most of my professional career as a manager working within an Information Technology (IT) area. During this time I often had responsibility over the email systems. Upon occasion, for other business reasons, my staff and I were asked to review emails. Upon doing so, we always seemed to come across people who sent personal emails via their work email. Most of them were totally innocent, such as telling their spouse they were working late. Some however, were complaining to their friends about their job, regarding sexual relations with other than their spouse, job hunting with other companies, and related to today's topic, racial and sexual oriented jokes. These findings were mostly kept private, unless they were illegal or against company policy. At minimum, these emails would be personally and/or professionally embarrassing. At worst, they could cost you your job or other dramatic personal loss.

The primary advice and takeaways from today's column is to know that:

- Off color jokes have a way of unexpectedly offending people

- Off color jokes must be kept out of the workplace, including email
- Just because you delete an email from your work email account, it doesn't mean that it's actually gone

For additional information on today's topic, I suggest the book *Making Diversity Work: 7 Steps for Defeating Bias in the Workplace* by Sondra Thiederman.

Until next time, manage well, manage smart, and continue to grow.

OFFICE GOSSIP ABOUT THE PEOPLE THAT
WORK FOR YOU

My suggestion is to not gossip at all. I know it can be fun. It can also be interesting to hear the gossip that is going around the office. The good news about gossip is it can help keep you in tune with what's going on around the company. The first lesson here is that it's fine to listen to gossip; it's not a good idea, however, to perpetuate it.

Next, there is an important distinction between gossiping about your peers and/or managers and gossiping about your staff. When you gossip about your peers, boss, or others, it is generally just taken as conjecture, because you presumably have no direct knowledge or official authority on the issue. When you gossip about your staff, it is taken by others as fact, not as gossip. The reason is it's your job to know what your staff is doing. So if you say it, it must be true.

A second reason not to gossip about your staff is because you're their manager. Your job is to protect your subordinates and treat them with respect. Would you want your manager to gossip about you?

Also, there are times when employees confide in their managers about health, family and personal problems that may affect their work. Discussing these personal items with other people is a breach of trust. Should you do so, you will hurt both your subordinate and yourself. Having this information disclosed hurts your subordinate. You have also hurt yourself by showing your staff, your peers, your boss, and the company that you are not trustworthy.

Think about things you may have confided to your boss

- During the interview process
- As a reason why you were late for a meeting
- Explaining why you needed work time off
- As a reason for your current poor performance on the job

How would you have liked it if your boss was passing that stuff around the office? Now put the shoe on the other foot with you as the manager.

This advice may sound very straight forward and easy to follow. But consider this question. Are there times when you must break an employee's confidence in an attempt to help them? Is this gossip or helping a friend? The answer is that it depends. This is where black and white turns into shades of gray. I'm by no means suggesting talking about a sensitive employee issue in the company cafeteria with your friends, that is definitely gossip and detrimental to your team member. I mean

- When asked, telling your boss that a staff member's performance is down because he/she is going through a bad divorce or medical issue
- What if your employee is being beaten up at home? Do you seek the help and guidance of Human Resources on what to do, or do you keep it private?
- When asked by another employee in your group, why it's ok for Jeff to leave early on Tuesdays and Thursday and he can't. Do you tell the person that Jeff is leaving early because he has cancer and is going to get radiation treatments?

These are very difficult questions to answer and certainly cannot be answered matter-of-fact like in this column. The key for you as a manager is to know when it's gossip and when it's business or human necessity. No one ever said being manager was easy, and sometimes it's really hard.

The primary advice and takeaways from today's column is to know that:

- Gossiping about staff is different than gossiping about your peers, it's much worse
- As a manager you should be protecting your staff, not gossiping about them; it hurts them and it hurts you

- Consider the question: Are there times when you must break an employee's confidence in an attempt to help them? If yes, is this gossip? Why or why not?

For additional information on today's topic, I suggest the book _The No Gossip Zone: A No-Nonsense Guide to a Healthy, High-Performing Work Environment_ by Sam Chapman.

Until next time, manage well, manage smart, and continue to grow.

FINAL THOUGHTS

As an author, trainer, speaker, and entrepreneur, when I read a management book—and there are many great books out there—my goals are always the same:

- To expand my knowledge of ideal management practices, techniques, and theories
- To deepen my understanding of what makes a great manager
- To learn how to be a better manager myself
- To assure that the information in my columns is theoretically strong, thought-provoking, and usable in the workplace

My hope for you, as a reader of this book and, hopefully, my future columns, is simply that you have found it valuable. Perhaps a few key points you encountered here will strengthen your abilities as a manager, a leader, and a person.

I would like to leave you with one last thought on management style. When writing a column every week for an extended period of time, you can't help but provide insights into your personal thoughts and philosophies on the topic. For me, as you may have surmised, I like to treat those who work for me fairly, honestly, and carefully. I have tried to help their careers, enhance their professional marketability, give them good things to work on, and provide a good work environment. As a result, most people who have worked for me once would work for me again. In fact, some have. That said, business is business, and as an employee myself, I have always tried to do the best I could for the company where I was employed. There are times when the goal of being an advocate for your staff and the goal of being an advocate for your company collide. As a result, there have been a few people that worked for me who strongly disagreed with decisions I made regarding their work assignments, performance reviews, and/or employment decisions. I always tried to do my best with/for these people. Sometimes I was successful, and, unfortunately, sometimes I failed. And across my career I have been on both sides of this coin—the employee and the manager.

The moral of this story is that you can't win them all. But if you truly try to do your best, for those reporting to you and for those to whom you report, you will look back on your career and feel you have:

- Won more than you have lost
- Acquired more professional friends than professional enemies
- Helped those around you achieve their professional goals
- Paid forward the help you have been given by helping others
- Tried your best
- Learned that your career, as a person and a manager, is a journey not a destination
- Enjoyed the ride

The interesting thing about writing a book that is a collection of ongoing smaller works is that the work continues after the book is published. At the time of this printing I have already written half the columns for my next book. These columns, listed in publication order, are:

- Playing favorites
- Start thinking like a CEO
- Have an open door policy? Make sure you're inside.
- Managers and Mentoring
- Setting team expectations
- Value of 360-degree analysis
- Work/Life Balance

- 8 questions that can help you improve your team's performance
- The Volunteer Manager
- Don't take the best people for granted
- 8 time management to-do tips for managers
- Making decisions using other people's expertise
- What does your office/cube say about you?
- Look for the invisible
- Bloom's Law on Technology Skill Set Marketability: Your current technology skill set has a two year half-life
- Being a player/coach in the workplace
- Embrace older workers
- Managers and knowledge-workers work in different time chunks
- Your friends come and go, but your enemies accumulate
- Celebrate your team's successes
- Making decisions using other people's expertise
- What Tai Chi taught me about being a manager
- 7 advantages of knowing your manager's constraints and limitations
- The 3 parts of every job
- Don't let the corporate nod happen to you
- What kind of manager are you? Do you know?
- Value of diversity within your team

If you don't want to wait for my next book to read these columns, they may be in your local GateHouse affiliate newspaper and/or in the archives of hundreds of GateHouse-related websites around the country.

As a final thought and request, if there is a topic you wish I had written about, please let me know. If I have the knowledge and can do the research, I'll try to write it. Truth be told, I would love your input. As I have said in the acknowledgements, my column readers make the writing worthwhile.

Thank you, manage well,
manage smart, and continue to grow.

Best wishes,
Eric